THE COMPLETE NINJA FOODI 2-BASKET AIR FRYER COOKBOOK

Deliciously Quick and Healthy Meals Cooked with DualZone Air Fryer Power | Full Color Edition

Judy K. Silas

Manufactured in the United States of America
Interior and Cover Designer: Danielle Rees
Art Producer: Brooke White
Editor: Aaliyah Lyons
Production Editor: Sienna Adams
Production Manager: Sarah Johnson
Photography: Michael Smith

TABLE OF CONTENTS

TABLE OF CONTENTS

TABLE OF CONTENTS

INTRODUCTION

When my friend first recommended the 2-Basket Ninja Foodi Air Fryer, I'll admit—I was skeptical. I've bought my fair share of kitchen gadgets that ended up collecting dust in the corner, gathering cobwebs. But something about her enthusiasm made me curious, so I decided to give it a go.

From the moment I took it out of the box, I was surprised by how easy it was to use. No complicated settings, no confusing buttons—just simple, intuitive controls. It was a game-changer in my kitchen. What really sold me, though, was how quickly it cooked meals and how deliciously crispy everything turned out. It wasn't just fast food; it was healthy, nutritious food that didn't make me feel guilty.

I found myself experimenting with all kinds of recipes—creating new flavors, perfecting textures, and finding ways to cook different dishes at once (thanks to the two baskets). It became a fun challenge, and soon I had a collection of recipes I was proud of. That's when I knew I had to share them with others. This book is the result of that journey—one that's made my life in the kitchen so much easier and tastier. I hope you'll enjoy these recipes as much as I have!

DEDICATION

To Della, I just wanted to thank you for introducing me to the Ninja Foodi 2-Basket Air Fryer. It's truly been a game-changer in my kitchen! I never imagined something so simple could make such a big difference in how I cook. The meals are quicker, healthier, and so delicious. I also treasure the memories of our vacations, cooking together and creating great meals. Those moments always bring me so much joy. I'm so grateful for your friendship and for sharing this wonderful kitchen tool with me. You always know how to make life more fun and flavorful!

CHAPTER1: MASTERING THE NINJA FOODI 2-BASKET AIR FRYER

WHY CHOOSE THE NINJA FOODI 2-BASKET AIR FRYER?

The Ninja Foodi 2-Basket Air Fryer has revolutionized home cooking with its thoughtful design and advanced technology. It offers versatility, time-saving convenience, and the ability to create healthier meals without sacrificing flavor. Here's an in-depth look at why it deserves a spot in your kitchen.

VERSATILITY: COOK MULTIPLE FOODS AT ONCE WITH THE TWO BASKETS

The two-basket design of the Ninja Foodi allows you to cook different dishes simultaneously, making it ideal for preparing complete meals in one go. Whether it's crispy chicken wings in one basket and seasoned potato wedges in the other, you can cater to different preferences and dietary needs without juggling multiple appliances.

Each basket operates independently, letting you choose separate cooking temperatures and times for each dish. This flexibility is perfect for creating balanced meals with a mix of proteins, vegetables, and sides. Additionally, it's a fantastic solution for meal prepping, allowing you to cook a variety of items at once for the week ahead. This level of versatility simplifies cooking, whether you're feeding a family or preparing meals for yourself.

TIME-SAVING: FASTER COOKING WITH EVEN RESULTS

The Ninja Foodi 2-Basket Air Fryer significantly cuts down cooking times compared to traditional methods. Its powerful fan technology ensures hot air circulates evenly around the food, reducing the overall time required for cooking. For example, items like chicken tenders, chips, or roasted vegetables cook in nearly half the time it would take in an oven.

This time-saving feature is especially beneficial for busy households or individuals who want to enjoy home-cooked meals without spending hours in the kitchen. With two baskets, you can prepare a main course and a side dish simultaneously, eliminating the need to cook in stages or wait for one dish to finish before starting another.

Reheating is another area where the Air Fryer excels. Leftovers like pizza, roasted vegetables, or fried chicken regain their original texture and crispness in minutes, offering a quicker and better alternative to traditional ovens or microwaves.

HEALTHIER MEALS: USE LESS OIL WITHOUT SACRIFICING TASTE

One of the standout benefits of the Ninja Foodi 2-Basket Air Fryer is its ability to create crispy, delicious meals with little to no oil. Instead of relying on deep-frying methods that submerge food in oil, this appliance uses hot air to achieve similar results. The outcome is golden, crispy foods that are significantly lower in fat and calories.

This feature makes it easier to enjoy traditionally unhealthy dishes, like chips or fried chicken, in a healthier way. For example, a batch of air-fried chips requires just a light spray of oil yet still achieves a crispy, satisfying texture. Similarly, breaded chicken or fish develops a crunchy coating without the need for excess oil.

The Air Fryer also enhances the nutritional value of meals by preserving the natural moisture and flavors of food. Proteins like salmon or chicken breasts stay tender and juicy, while vegetables retain their nutrients and develop a delicious roasted flavor.

Additionally, its ability to roast, bake, and dehydrate expands your options for preparing healthy snacks and meals. From roasted nuts and dried fruits to baked sweet potato wedges, the possibilities are endless, ensuring you can maintain a healthy diet without compromising on taste or variety.

HOW TO USE YOUR NINJA FOODI 2-BASKET AIR FRYER

The Ninja Foodi 2-Basket Air Fryer is designed to simplify your cooking process while delivering delicious results. Here's a comprehensive guide on how to get started, master its features, and make the most of its dual baskets.

SIMPLE CONTROLS: INTUITIVE SETTINGS FOR EASY OPERATION

The Ninja Foodi 2-Basket Air Fryer is equipped with an easy-to-use control panel that makes operating it straightforward, even for beginners. Once plugged in, you'll find clear labels and buttons for each function. The display includes temperature, time, and cooking mode indicators, providing all the information you need at a glance.

Start by selecting the basket you want to use, as each has its own set of controls. If you're cooking in both baskets, set the temperature and time for each individually. The fryer's buttons allow you to toggle between air fry, roast, bake, reheat, and dehydrate modes, depending on your recipe. Simply adjust the temperature and time using the "+" and "−" buttons to ensure precision.

The controls also include a pause feature, so you can check on your food mid-cooking without disrupting the process. This is particularly useful for ensuring even results or adding additional seasoning partway through cooking. With its intuitive design, mastering the Ninja Foodi's controls only takes a few uses.

OPTIMIZING COOKING MODES FOR DIFFERENT MEALS

The Ninja Foodi offers multiple cooking modes, each tailored to deliver the best results for different types of meals. Learning how to use these modes effectively can elevate your cooking experience.

- **Air Fry Mode:** Perfect for achieving a crispy texture on items like fries, wings, and breaded fish. This mode uses rapid hot air circulation, which requires little to no oil. For best results, lightly coat your food in oil or breadcrumbs to enhance crispness.

- **Roast Mode:** Ideal for meats, vegetables, and baked goods. This setting provides consistent heat that mimics the effects of an oven, ensuring a tender inside with a perfectly roasted exterior. Use this mode for dishes like roasted chicken or baked potatoes.

- **Reheat Mode:** A lifesaver for leftovers. This mode restores the original texture and flavor of foods like pizza, fried chicken, or roasted veggies without the sogginess that microwaves often cause.

- **Dehydrate Mode:** Best for making healthy snacks like dried fruits, vegetable chips, or beef jerky. This low-heat setting removes moisture without cooking the food, preserving its nutritional value and extending shelf life.

When switching between modes, always ensure your temperature and time settings align with your specific recipe. The user manual provides a helpful guide for common foods, but feel free to experiment and adjust settings based on your preferences.

COOKING TIPS: MAXIMISING THE USE OF BOTH BASKETS

To make the most of your Ninja Foodi 2-Basket Air Fryer, focus on efficient use of its dual baskets. This feature allows you to prepare a main dish and side simultaneously, saving time and effort. For example, cook chicken in one basket while roasting vegetables in the other. Both items will be ready to serve at the same time, ensuring a seamless meal preparation process.

Use the size of the baskets to your advantage. Foods like chips, wings, or vegetables should be spread out evenly in a single layer to ensure even airflow and consistent results. Overloading the baskets may result in uneven cooking, so it's better to cook in batches if you have larger quantities.

Finally, always pre-cut or prepare your ingredients before placing them in the fryer. For instance, slice vegetables into uniform sizes to promote even cooking and seasoning. Lightly toss items in oil or seasoning before air frying for added flavor and crispness. Cleaning the baskets between uses also helps maintain optimal performance and prevents cross-contamination of flavors.

TIPS FOR BEGINNERS

Starting with the Ninja Foodi 2-Basket Air Fryer can be an exciting journey into faster, healthier, and tastier cooking. Here are some practical tips to help beginners make the most of this versatile appliance.

START WITH BASIC RECIPES TO GET COMFORTABLE

If you're new to air frying, begin with simple recipes to familiarize yourself with the appliance and its capabilities. Classics like fries, roasted vegetables, or chicken tenders are great starting points. These recipes typically require minimal preparation and give you a chance to understand how the air fryer works.

Pay attention to the suggested cooking times and temperatures in the manual or recipes. While these provide a reliable baseline, you may need to adjust slightly depending on the thickness of your food or your preferred level of crispiness. Starting simple allows you to experiment without feeling overwhelmed, gradually building your confidence to try more complex dishes.

PREHEAT THE AIR FRYER FOR BEST RESULTS

While the Ninja Foodi 2-Basket Air Fryer heats up quickly, preheating it before placing your food inside can significantly enhance cooking results. Preheating ensures the baskets reach the desired temperature before cooking begins, helping food to cook more evenly and achieve a golden, crispy texture.

Preheating is especially important for recipes requiring precise temperature control, like baked goods or proteins. Most air fryers, including this model, allow you to preheat by running the appliance empty for a few minutes at the target temperature. Once preheated, quickly place your food in the basket and start cooking. This step may seem small, but it can make a noticeable difference in your final results.

CLEAN AND MAINTAIN YOUR AIR FRYER FOR LONGEVITY

Regular cleaning and maintenance are key to keeping your air fryer in excellent working condition for years to come. After each use, allow the appliance to cool completely before cleaning. Remove the baskets and wash them with warm, soapy water or place them in the dishwasher if they're dishwasher-safe. Avoid using abrasive sponges, as they can damage the non-stick coating.

For the interior of the air fryer, wipe down the surfaces with a damp cloth to remove any food residue. Periodically check the heating elements for buildup and clean them gently if needed. Proper maintenance not only extends the life of your air fryer but also ensures consistent performance and avoids transferring unwanted flavors to your food.

Air Fryer Cooking Chart

Beef

Item	Temp (°F)	Time (mins)	Item	Temp (°F)	Time (mins)
Beef Eye Round Roast (4 lbs.)	400 °F	45 to 55	Meatballs (1-inch)	370 °F	7
Burger Patty (4 oz.)	370 °F	16 to 20	Meatballs (3-inch)	380 °F	10
Filet Mignon (8 oz.)	400 °F	18	Ribeye, bone-in (1-inch, 8 oz)	400 °F	10 to 15
Flank Steak (1.5 lbs.)	400 °F	12	Sirloin steaks (1-inch, 12 oz)	400 °F	9 to 14
Flank Steak (2 lbs.)	400 °F	20 to 28			

Chicken

Item	Temp (°F)	Time (mins)	Item	Temp (°F)	Time (mins)
Breasts, bone in (1 ¼ lb.)	370 °F	25	Legs, bone-in (1 ¾ lb.)	380 °F	30
Breasts, boneless (4 oz)	380 °F	12	Thighs, boneless (1 ½ lb.)	380 °F	18 to 20
Drumsticks (2 ½ lb.)	370 °F	20	Wings (2 lb.)	400 °F	12
Game Hen (halved 2 lb.)	390 °F	20	Whole Chicken	360 °F	75
Thighs, bone-in (2 lb.)	380 °F	22	Tenders	360 °F	8 to 10

Pork & Lamb

Item	Temp (°F)	Time (mins)	Item	Temp (°F)	Time (mins)
Bacon (regular)	400 °F	5 to 7	Pork Tenderloin	370 °F	15
Bacon (thick cut)	400 °F	6 to 10	Sausages	380 °F	15
Pork Loin (2 lb.)	360 °F	55	Lamb Loin Chops (1-inch thick)	400 °F	8 to 12
Pork Chops, bone in (1-inch, 6.5 oz)	400 °F	12	Rack of Lamb (1.5 – 2 lb.)	380 °F	22

Fish & Seafood

Item	Temp (°F)	Time (mins)	Item	Temp (°F)	Time (mins)
Calamari (8 oz)	400 °F	4	Tuna Steak	400 °F	7 to 10
Fish Fillet (1-inch, 8 oz)	400 °F	10	Scallops	400 °F	5 to 7
Salmon, fillet (6 oz)	380 °F	12	Shrimp	400 °F	5
Swordfish steak	400 °F	10			

Air Fryer Cooking Chart

Vegetables					
INGREDIENT	AMOUNT	PREPARATION	OIL	TEMP	COOK TIME
Asparagus	2 bunches	Cut in half, trim stems	2 Tbsp	420°F	12-15 mins
Beets	1½ lbs	Peel, cut in ½-inch cubes	1Tbsp	390°F	28-30 mins
Bell peppers (for roasting)	4 peppers	Cut in quarters, remove seeds	1Tbsp	400°F	15-20 mins
Broccoli	1 large head	Cut in 1-2-inch florets	1Tbsp	400°F	15-20 mins
Brussels sprouts	1lb	Cut in half, remove stems	1Tbsp	425°F	15-20 mins
Carrots	1lb	Peel, cut in ¼-inch rounds	1 Tbsp	425°F	10-15 mins
Cauliflower	1 head	Cut in 1-2-inch florets	2 Tbsp	400°F	20-22 mins
Corn on the cob	7 ears	Whole ears, remove husks	1 Tbps	400°F	14-17 mins
Green beans	1 bag (12 oz)	Trim	1 Tbps	420°F	18-20 mins
Kale (for chips)	4 oz	Tear into pieces,remove stems	None	325°F	5-8 mins
Mushrooms	16 oz	Rinse, slice thinly	1 Tbps	390°F	25-30 mins
Potatoes, russet	1½ lbs	Cut in 1-inch wedges	1 Tbps	390°F	25-30 mins
Potatoes, russet	1lb	Hand-cut fries, soak 30 mins in cold water, then pat dry	½ -3 Tbps	400°F	25-28 mins
Potatoes, sweet	1lb	Hand-cut fries, soak 30 mins in cold water, then pat dry	1 Tbps	400°F	25-28 mins
Zucchini	1lb	Cut in eighths lengthwise, then cut in half	1 Tbps	400°F	15-20 mins

CHAPTER 2:
APPETIZERS AND
SNACKS RECIPES

POTATO TATER TOTS

Prep time: **10 minutes** | Cook time: **27 minutes** | Serves **4**

- 2 potatoes, peeled
- ½ teaspoon Cajun seasoning
- Olive oil cooking spray
- Sea salt to taste

1. Boil water in a cooking pot and cook potatoes in it for 15 minutes.
2. Drain and leave the potatoes to cool in a bowl.
3. Grate these potatoes and toss them with Cajun seasoning.
4. Make small tater tots out of this mixture.
5. Divide them into the two crisper plates and spray them with cooking oil.
6. Return the crisper plates to the Ninja Foodi 2-Basket Air Fryer.
7. Choose the Air Fry mode for Basket 1 and set the temperature to 375 °F and the time to 27 minutes.
8. Select the "MATCH" button to copy the settings for Basket 2.
9. Initiate cooking by pressing the START/STOP button.
10. Flip them once cooked halfway through, and resume cooking.
11. Serve warm

MOZZARELLA STICKS

Prep time: **1 hour 10 minutes** | Cook time: **1 hour 15 minutes** | Serves **8**

- 8 mozzarella sticks
- ¼ cup all-purpose flour
- 1 egg, whisked
- 1 cup panko breadcrumbs
- ½ teaspoon each onion powder, garlic powder, smoked paprika, salt

1. Freeze the mozzarella sticks for 30 minutes after placing them on a parchment-lined plate.
2. Fill a Ziploc bag halfway with flour. In a small dish, whisk the egg. In a separate shallow bowl, combine the panko and spices.
3. Toss the sticks into the bag of flour, seal it, and shake to coat the cheese evenly. Take out the sticks and dip them in the egg, then in the panko, one at a time. Put the coated sticks back on the plate and put them in the freezer for another 30 minutes.
4. Place a crisper plate in each drawer, then add the mozzarella sticks in a single layer to each. Insert the drawers into the unit.
5. Select basket 1, then AIR FRY, then set the temperature to 400 °F with a 15-minute timer. To match basket 2 settings to basket 1, choose MATCH. Press START/STOP to begin the cooking process.

CAULIFLOWER POPPERS

Prep time: 15 minutes | Cook time: 20 minutes | Serves 6

- 3 tablespoons olive oil
- 1 teaspoon paprika
- ⅛ teaspoon cayenne pepper
- ½ teaspoon ground cumin
- ¼ teaspoon ground turmeric
- Salt and ground black pepper, as required
- 1 medium head cauliflower, cut into florets

1. Press "Basket 1" and "Basket 2" of Ninja Foodi 2-Basket Air Fryer and then rotate the knob for each basket to select "Bake".
2. Set the temperature to 450 °F for both baskets and then set the time for 5 minutes to preheat.
3. In a bowl, place all ingredients and toss to coat well.
4. Divide the cauliflower mixture into 2 greased baking pans.
5. After preheating, arrange 1 baking pan into the basket of each basket.
6. Slide each basket into Air Fryer and set the time for 20 minutes.
7. While cooking, flip the cauliflower mixture once halfway through.
8. After cooking time is completed, remove the baking pans from Air Fryer and serve the cauliflower poppers warm.

PUMPKIN FRIES

Prep time: 25 minutes | Cook time: 15 minutes | Serves 4

- ½ cup plain Greek yoghurt
- 2 to 3 teaspoons minced chipotle peppers
- ⅛ teaspoon plus ½ teaspoon salt, divided
- 1 medium pie pumpkin
- ¼ teaspoon garlic powder
- ¼ teaspoon ground cumin
- ¼ teaspoon chilli powder
- ¼ teaspoon pepper

1. Combine yoghurt, chipotle peppers, and ⅛ teaspoon salt in a small bowl. Refrigerate until ready to serve, covered.
2. Peeled the pumpkin and split it in half lengthwise. Discard the seeds. Cut pumpkin into ½-inch strips.
3. Place in a large mixing bowl. Toss with ½ teaspoon salt, garlic powder, cumin, chilli powder, and pepper.
4. Press "Basket 1" and "Basket 2" and then rotate the knob for each zone to select "Air Fry".
5. Set the temperature to 400 °F for both zones, and then set the time for 5 minutes to preheat.
6. After preheating, spray the Air-Fryer basket of each zone with cooking spray and line them with parchment paper. Arrange pumpkin fries and spritz cooking spray on them.
7. Slide the basket into Air Fryer and set the time for 8 minutes.
8. After that, toss them and again cook for 3 minutes longer.
9. After cooking time is completed, transfer them onto serving plates and serve.

ONION RINGS

Prep time: **5 minutes** | Cook time: **10 minutes** |Serves **4**

- 1 cup all-purpose flour
- 1 tablespoon seasoned salt
- 1 cup whole milk
- 1 large egg
- 1 cup panko bread crumbs
- 1 large Vidalia onion, peeled and sliced into ¼"-thick rings

1. Preheat the air fryer to 350°F.
2. In a large bowl, whisk together the flour and seasoned salt.
3. In a medium bowl, whisk together the milk and egg.
4. Place the bread crumbs in a separate large bowl.
5. Dip the onion rings into the flour mixture, ensuring they are evenly coated, then set them aside.
6. Pour the milk mixture into the bowl with the flour and stir to combine.
7. Dip the floured onion rings into the wet mixture and then press into the panko bread crumbs to coat.
8. Divide the onion rings into two baskets:
   - Basket 1: Place half of the coated onion rings in the first basket in a single layer.
   - Basket 2: Place the remaining onion rings in the second basket in a similar manner.
9. Cook both baskets at 350°F for 10 minutes, shaking both baskets halfway through the cooking time for even crisping. The onion rings should be golden, crispy on the edges, and tender inside.
10. Once cooked, serve the onion rings immediately, hot and crispy!

SWEET-AND-SALTY PRETZELS

Prep time: 5 minutes | **Cook time: 5 minutes** | **Serves 4**

- 2 cups Plain pretzel nuggets
- 1 tablespoon Worcestershire sauce
- 2 teaspoons Granulated white sugar
- 1 teaspoon Mild smoked paprika
- ½ teaspoon Garlic or onion powder

1. Preheat the air fryer to 350°F.
2. In a large bowl, toss the pretzel nuggets, Worcestershire sauce, sugar, smoked paprika, and garlic (or onion) powder until the nuggets are well coated.
3. Divide the pretzels into two baskets:
   - Basket 1: Place half of the pretzel mixture into one of the baskets, spreading the nuggets into a single layer as much as possible.
   - Basket 2: Place the remaining pretzels in the second basket in a similar manner.
4. Cook both baskets at 350°F for 5 minutes. Shake both baskets halfway through the cooking time to ensure the pretzels are evenly toasted. The pretzels are done when they are golden, aromatic, and crispy. Watch carefully to ensure they don't burn, especially if your air fryer is set to a higher temperature, like 360°F.
5. Once cooked, pour the pretzels from both baskets onto a wire rack, spreading them into a single layer. Let them cool for 5 minutes before serving.

AVOCADO FRIES WITH SRIRACHA DIP

Prep time: 10 minutes | **Cook time: 6 minutes** | **Serves 4**

- 4 avocados, peeled and cut into sticks
- ¾ cup panko breadcrumbs
- ¼ cup flour
- 2 eggs, beaten
- ½ teaspoon garlic powder
- ½ teaspoon salt
- ¼ cup ranch dressing
- 1 teaspoon sriracha sauce

1. Mix flour with garlic powder and salt in a bowl.
2. Dredge the avocado sticks through the flour mixture.
3. Dip them in the eggs and coat them with breadcrumbs.
4. Place the coated fries in the air fryer baskets.
5. Return the air fryer basket 1 to Basket 1, and basket 2 to Basket 2 of the Ninja Foodi 2-Basket Air Fryer.
6. Choose the "Air Fry" mode for Basket 1 at 400 °F and 6 minutes of cooking time.
7. Select the "MATCH COOK" option to copy the settings for Basket 2.
8. Initiate cooking by pressing the START/PAUSE BUTTON.
9. Flip the fries once cooked halfway through.
10. Mix all the dipping sauce ingredients in a bowl.
11. Serve the fries with dipping sauce.

CRISPY PLANTAIN CHIPS WITH SPICY TORTILLA STRIPS

Prep time: **15 minutes** | Cook time: **20 minutes** | Serves **4**

Basket 1 - Crispy Plantain Chips:
- 1 green plantain
- 1 teaspoon canola oil
- ½ teaspoon sea salt

Basket 2 - Spicy Tortilla Strips:
- 2 corn tortillas
- 1 tablespoon olive oil
- ½ teaspoon chili powder
- ¼ teaspoon garlic powder
- Pinch of salt

1. Peel and cut the plantains into long, thin strips using a mandolin slicer.
2. Cut corn tortillas into thin strips for the second basket.
3. Grease the crisper plates with ½ teaspoon of canola oil for Basket 1.
4. Toss the plantains with salt and remaining canola oil in Basket 1.
5. In Basket 2, toss tortilla strips with olive oil, chili powder, garlic powder, and salt.
6. Return the crisper plates to the Ninja Foodi 2-Basket Air Fryer.
7. Choose the Air Fry mode for Basket 1 and set the temperature to 350°F for 20 minutes.
8. Select the "MATCH" button to copy the settings for Basket 2.
9. Initiate cooking by pressing the START/STOP button.
10. Toss the plantains in Basket 1 and shake the tortilla strips in Basket 2 after 10 minutes.
11. Continue cooking until both are crispy and golden.
12. Serve warm.

FRIED OKRA

Prep time: **5 minutes** | Cook time: **10 minutes** |Serves **4**

- 1-pound fresh okra
- 1 cup buttermilk
- 1 cup all-purpose flour
- 1 cup cornmeal
- 1 teaspoon kosher salt
- 1 teaspoon fresh ground pepper

1. Wash and trim the ends of the okra before slicing it into 12-inch chunks.
2. In a small dish, pour the buttermilk.
3. Combine flour, cornmeal, salt, and pepper in a separate dish.
4. Coat all sides of okra slices in buttermilk and then in flour mixture.
5. Place a baking sheet on the baskets.
6. Press "Basket 1" and "Basket 2" and then rotate the knob for each zone to select "Air Fryer".
7. Set the temperature to 350 °F for both zones, and then set the time for 5 minutes to preheat.
8. After preheating, arrange them into the basket of each zone.
9. Slide the baskets into Air Fryer and set the time for 8 minutes.
10. After cooking time is completed, place on a wire rack for a few minutes, then transfer onto serving plates and serve.

BALSAMIC ROASTED GRAPES WITH CRISPY ROSEMARY CHICKPEA CHIPS

Prep time: **5 minutes** | Cook time: **25 minutes** | Serves **6**

Basket 1 - Balsamic Roasted Grapes and Yogurt Dip:
- 2 cups seedless red grapes
- 1 tbsp balsamic vinegar
- 1 tbsp honey
- 1 cup Greek yogurt
- 2 tbsp milk
- 2 tbsp minced fresh basil

Basket 2 - Crispy Rosemary Chickpea Chips:
- 1 can chickpeas, drained and dried
- 2 tbsp olive oil
- 1 tsp dried
- rosemary
- ½ tsp garlic powder
- Salt to taste

1. Preheat your Ninja Foodi 2-Basket Air Fryer to 380°F.
2. For Balsamic Grapes: Add the grapes to Basket 1. Drizzle balsamic vinegar and honey over the grapes, then toss gently to coat them evenly with the mixture.
3. For Chickpea Chips: Pat the chickpeas completely dry with a paper towel to remove excess moisture. In Basket 2, toss the chickpeas with olive oil, rosemary, garlic powder, and salt, ensuring they are well coated.
4. Air fry both baskets at 380°F: Roast the grapes for 8-12 minutes, or until they become slightly shriveled. Meanwhile, crisp the chickpeas for 15-20 minutes, shaking the basket every 5 minutes to ensure even cooking.
5. Once the grapes are done, remove them from Basket 1 and let them cool slightly.
6. In a separate bowl, mix together the milk and yogurt. Gently stir the roasted grapes and minced basil into the yogurt mixture.
7. Serve the balsamic grape yogurt dip alongside the crispy rosemary chickpea chips for dipping.

CHAPTER 3: BREAKFAST RECIPES

BREAKFAST BAKE

Prep time: **5 minutes** | Cook time: **15 minutes** |Serves **4**

- 6 large eggs
- 2 tablespoons heavy cream
- ½ teaspoon salt
- ¼ teaspoon ground black pepper
- 1/3 pound ground pork breakfast sausage, cooked and drained
- ½ cup shredded Cheddar cheese

For the Bacon (Basket 2):
- 6 slices of bacon

1. Preheat the air fryer to 320°F. Lightly spray a 6" round cake pan with cooking spray.
2. In a large bowl, whisk the eggs, heavy cream, salt, and black pepper until fully combined.
3. Arrange the cooked sausage in the bottom of the prepared pan. Pour the egg mixture over the sausage and then sprinkle the shredded Cheddar cheese on top.
4. Place the pan into Basket 1 of the air fryer. Cook at 320°F for 15 minutes or until the top begins to brown and the center is set.
5. Lay 6 slices of bacon in Basket 2.
6. Cook at 320°F for 10-12 minutes, flipping halfway through, until crispy and browned.
7. Let the breakfast bake cool for 5 minutes before slicing. Serve warm, alongside the crispy bacon.

EASY SCONES

Prep time: **5 minutes** | Cook time: **8 minutes per batch** | Serves **9**

- 2 cups self-rising flour, plus ¼ cup for kneading
- ⅓ cup granulated sugar
- ¼ cup butter, cold
- 1 cup milk

1. Preheat the Ninja Foodi 2-Basket Air Fryer to 360°F.
2. In a large bowl, stir together the flour and sugar.
3. Cut the cold butter into tiny cubes, then stir into the flour mixture with a fork until it resembles breadcrumbs.
4. Stir in the milk gradually, mixing until a soft dough forms.
5. Sprinkle ¼ cup of flour onto a piece of wax paper and place the dough on top.
6. Lightly knead the dough by folding and turning it 6 to 8 times.
7. Pat the dough into a 6 x 6-inch square.
8. Cut the dough into 9 equal squares.
9. For Basket 1: Place half of the scones in the air fryer basket, close together but not touching (you can also place them in a baking pan that fits inside the basket).
10. For Basket 2: Place the remaining scones in the second basket.
11. Place Basket 1 and Basket 2 into the air fryer and cook at 360°F for 8 minutes. The scones will be lightly browned on top and will spring back when pressed gently with a dull knife.
12. If there are any scones left to cook, repeat steps 7 and 8 until all the scones are cooked.

STRAWBERRY BREAD WITH CRISPY BACON OR SAUSAGES

Prep time: 5 minutes | Cook time: 28 minutes | Serves 6

- ½ cup frozen strawberries in juice, completely thawed (do not drain)
- 1 cup flour
- ½ cup sugar
- 1 teaspoon
- cinnamon
- ½ teaspoon baking soda
- ⅛ teaspoon salt
- 1 egg, beaten
- ⅓ cup oil
- Cooking spray

Crispy Bacon or Sausages (for Basket 2):

- 6 slices of bacon or 4 sausages

1. Cut any large strawberries into smaller pieces, no larger than ½ inch.
2. Preheat the Ninja Foodi 2-Basket Air Fryer to 330°F.
3. In a large bowl, stir together the flour, sugar, cinnamon, baking soda, and salt.
4. In a small bowl, mix together the egg, oil, and the thawed strawberries. Add the wet mixture to the dry ingredients and stir gently until combined.
5. Spray a 6 x 6-inch baking pan with cooking spray to prevent sticking.
6. Pour the batter into the prepared pan.
7. Place the pan in Basket 1 and cook at 330°F for 28 minutes. The bread is done when a toothpick inserted in the centre comes out clean.
8. Lay 6 slices of bacon or 4 sausages in Basket 2.
9. Cook at 330°F for 10-12 minutes, flipping halfway, until crispy and browned.
10. When the bread is done, let it cool in the pan for 10 minutes before removing it.
11. Serve with your crispy bacon or sausages for a complete breakfast or snack.

CRISPY BACON & GOLDEN HASH BROWNS

Prep time: 5 minutes | Cook time: 20 minutes |Serves 2

- 6 rashers of smoked bacon
- 2 medium-sized potatoes (peeled and grated)
- 1 tbsp olive oil (or vegetable oil)
- Salt and pepper, to taste
- ½ tsp garlic powder (optional)
- Fresh parsley, finely chopped (optional, for garnish)

1. Preheat your Ninja Foodi 2-Basket Air Fryer to 200°C (180°C for fan-assisted).
2. Place the rashers of bacon in Basket 1, laying them flat. You may need to trim the bacon to fit, depending on the size of your baskets.
3. Air fry the bacon at 200°C for 10-12 minutes, flipping halfway through. Adjust the time for crispiness according to your preference.
4. While the bacon cooks, prepare the hash browns. Place the grated potatoes into a clean kitchen towel or cheesecloth, and wring out as much moisture as possible.
5. In a mixing bowl, combine the dry grated potatoes, olive oil, salt, pepper, and garlic powder (if using). Stir well to coat the potatoes evenly.
6. Place the potato mixture into Basket 2. Use a spoon to spread it out into a flat, even layer.
7. Air fry at 200°C for 15-18 minutes, shaking the basket halfway through, until the hash browns are golden brown and crispy.

MORNING PATTIES

Prep time: **15 minutes** | Cook time: **20 minutes** |Serves **4**

- 1 lb. minced pork
- 1 lb. minced turkey
- 2 teaspoons dry rubbed sage
- 2 teaspoons fennel seeds
- 2 teaspoons garlic powder
- 1 teaspoon paprika
- 1 teaspoon of sea salt
- 1 teaspoon dried thyme

1. In a mixing bowl, combine the minced pork and minced turkey, mixing them together until well incorporated.
2. In a small bowl, mix the sage, fennel seeds, garlic powder, paprika, sea salt, and dried thyme.
3. Drizzle the seasoning mixture over the meat and mix thoroughly until the spices are evenly distributed.
4. Take 2 tablespoons of the meat mixture at a time and roll them into thick patties.
5. Place half of the patties in Basket 1 and the other half in Basket 2. Lightly spray the patties with cooking oil.
6. Insert the crisper plate back into the Ninja Foodi 2-Basket Air Fryer.
7. Set the air fryer to 390°F for 13 minutes in Basket 1.
8. Press the "MATCH" button to copy the settings to Basket 2.
9. Press START/STOP to begin cooking. Flip the patties halfway through cooking to ensure even browning on both sides.
10. Once cooked, remove the patties from both baskets and serve them warm and fresh.

SCRAMBLED EGGS & SAUTÉED MUSHROOMS

Prep time: **5 minutes** | Cook time: **20 minutes** |Serves **2**

- 4 large eggs
- 1 tbsp butter
- ½ tsp salt
- ¼ tsp black pepper
- 7 oz button mushrooms, sliced
- 1 tbsp olive oil

1. Preheat the Ninja Foodi 2-Basket Air Fryer to 360°F for about 3-5 minutes.
2. Crack the eggs into a bowl.
3. Whisk the eggs with the salt and pepper until fully combined and slightly frothy.
4. Add the butter to a small ovenproof dish or an air fryer-safe pan that fits in Basket 1.
5. Pour the egg mixture over the butter in the pan, ensuring it spreads out evenly.
6. Clean and slice the mushrooms.
7. In a mixing bowl, toss the sliced mushrooms with olive oil, salt, and pepper, making sure the mushrooms are well coated.
8. Place the dish with the scrambled egg mixture into Basket 1.
9. Spread the seasoned mushrooms evenly in Basket 2.
10. Set both baskets to 360°F and air fry for 10-12 minutes.
11. After 5 minutes, open the air fryer and stir the scrambled eggs in Basket 1 to ensure they cook evenly. The eggs will start to form curds, so use a spoon or spatula to gently stir them.
12. Continue cooking both baskets for the remaining time (about 5-7 minutes).
13. Check the mushrooms in Basket 2 around the 8-minute mark. They should be tender and lightly browned. Shake the basket halfway through to ensure even cooking.
14. Once the eggs are scrambled and soft (but not overcooked), and the mushrooms are golden and tender, remove both baskets.
15. Serve the scrambled eggs alongside the sautéed mushrooms.

SPINACH OMELET WITH CRISPY BACON

Prep time: 5 minutes | Cook time: 12 minutes |Serves 2

- 4 large eggs
- 1½ cups chopped fresh spinach leaves
- 2 tablespoons peeled and chopped yellow onion
- 2 tablespoons salted butter, melted
- ½ cup shredded mild Cheddar cheese
- ¼ teaspoon salt

For Basket 2 (Side Option):
- 4 slices of bacon

1. In an ungreased 6-inch round nonstick baking dish, whisk the eggs. Stir in the chopped spinach, onion, melted butter, shredded Cheddar cheese, and salt. Mix until well combined.
2. Place the baking dish into Basket 1 and set the temperature to 320°F. Cook for 12 minutes, or until the omelet is browned on top and firm in the centre. If needed, check for doneness and cook for a couple more minutes.
3. Place 4 slices of bacon in Basket 2. Cook at 320°F for 6-8 minutes, flipping halfway through, until crispy and golden brown.
4. Once the omelet is done, slice it in half and serve on two medium plates. Add the crispy bacon on the side for a complete meal.

MORNING EGG ROLLS

Prep time: 15 minutes | Cook time: 13 minutes |Serves 6

- 2 eggs
- 2 tablespoons milk
- Salt, to taste
- Black pepper, to taste
- ½ cup shredded cheddar cheese
- 2 sausage patties
- 6 egg roll wrappers
- 1 tablespoon olive oil
- 1 cup water

1. Grease a small skillet with some olive oil and place it over medium heat.
2. Add sausage patties and cook them until brown.
3. Chop the cooked patties into small pieces. Beat eggs with salt, black pepper, and milk in a mixing bowl.
4. Grease the same skillet with 1 teaspoon of olive oil and pour the egg mixture into it.
5. Stir cook to make scrambled eggs.
6. Add sausage, mix well and remove the skillet from the heat.
7. Spread an egg roll wrapper on the working surface in a diamond shape position.
8. Add a tablespoon of cheese at the bottom third of the roll wrapper.
9. Top the cheese with egg mixture and wet the edges of the wrapper with water.
10. Fold the two corners of the wrapper and roll it, then seal the edges.
11. Repeat the same steps and divide the rolls in the two crisper plates.
12. Return the crisper plates to the Ninja Foodi 2-Basket Air Fryer.
13. Choose the Air Fry mode for Basket 1 and set the temperature to 375 °F and the time to 13 minutes.
14. Select the "MATCH" button to copy the settings for Basket 2.
15. Initiate cooking by pressing the START/STOP button.
16. Flip the rolls after 8 minutes and continue cooking for another 5 minutes.
17. Serve warm and fresh.

WHOLE-GRAIN CORNBREAD WITH ROASTED VEGETABLES

Prep time: **5 minutes** | Cook time: **25 minutes** | Serves **6**

- 1 cup stoneground cornmeal
- ½ cup brown rice flour
- 1 teaspoon sugar
- 2 teaspoons baking powder
- ¼ teaspoon salt
- 1 cup milk
- 2 tablespoons oil
- 2 eggs
- Cooking spray

For Basket 2 (Side Option):
- 1 cup mixed vegetables (e.g., carrots, bell peppers, and zucchini)
- 1 tablespoon olive oil
- Salt and pepper to taste

1. In a medium mixing bowl, combine the cornmeal, brown rice flour, sugar, baking powder, and salt.
2. Add the milk, oil, and eggs, and stir until the batter is smooth.
3. Spray the air fryer baking pan with nonstick cooking spray and pour the cornbread batter into the pan.
4. Place the baking pan into Basket 1 of the air fryer.
5. Toss the mixed vegetables with olive oil, salt, and pepper.
6. Place the seasoned vegetables into Basket 2.
7. Set the temperature to 360°F.
8. Cook the cornbread for 25 minutes or until the center is firm and a toothpick comes out clean.
9. At the same time, cook the vegetables in Basket 2 for 15-20 minutes at the same temperature, stirring halfway through, until the vegetables are tender and slightly browned.
10. Once done, remove both baskets. Allow the cornbread to cool slightly before slicing. Serve the cornbread with the roasted vegetables on the side.

CHAPTER 4: POULTRY MAINS RECIPES

SPINACH & TURKEY MEATBALLS

Prep time: **5 minutes** | Cook time: **45 minutes** | Serves **4**

- ¼ cup grated Parmesan cheese
- 2 scallions, chopped
- 1 garlic clove, minced
- 1 egg, beaten
- 1 cup baby spinach, chopped
- ¼ cup bread crumbs
- 1 tsp dried oregano
- Salt and pepper, to taste
- 1 ¼ lb ground turkey

1. Preheat the air fryer to 400°F and the oven to 250°F to keep the meatballs warm after cooking.
2. In a large bowl, combine the chopped scallions, minced garlic, beaten egg, chopped spinach, bread crumbs, Parmesan cheese, oregano, salt, and pepper. Mix everything together until well combined.
3. Add the ground turkey to the mixture and mix until fully incorporated. Roll the mixture into 1½-inch meatballs.
4. Basket 1: Place the first batch of meatballs into Basket 1, making sure they fit in a single layer.
5. Basket 2: Place the second batch of meatballs into Basket 2, also in a single layer.
6. Air Fry both baskets at 400°F for 10-15 minutes, shaking each basket halfway through the cooking time (around minute 7) for even cooking.
7. Once cooked, transfer the meatballs to a baking tray and cover with foil to keep them warm in the oven set to 250°F.
8. Repeat the process with any remaining meatballs, using both baskets to cook in parallel for a quicker result.
9. Once all meatballs are cooked, serve warm with your favourite side or sauce.

LEMON HERB WHOLE CORNISH HEN

Prep time: **5 minutes** | Cook time: **50 minutes** | Serves **2**

- 1 Cornish hen
- ¼ cup olive oil
- 2 tbsp lemon juice
- 2 tbsp sage, chopped
- 2 tbsp thyme, chopped
- 4 garlic cloves, chopped
- Salt and pepper, to taste
- 1 celery stalk, chopped
- ½ small onion, chopped
- ½ lemon, juiced and zested
- 2 tbsp chopped parsley

1. Preheat the air fryer to 380°F.
2. In a bowl, whisk together the olive oil, lemon juice, sage, thyme, chopped garlic, salt, and pepper.
3. Rub the herb mixture generously over the top and sides of the Cornish hen. Pour any excess mixture inside the cavity of the bird for extra flavour.
4. Stuff the celery, onion, and lemon juice and zest into the cavity of the hen for added moisture and flavour.
5. Place the Cornish hen in Basket 1 of your air fryer.
6. To speed up cooking, place the celery, onion, and lemon mixture in Basket 2 and air-fry them to create a delicious side.
7. Roast both at 380°F for 40-45 minutes, flipping the hen halfway through the cooking time for even browning. The hen is done when its internal temperature reaches 165°F.
8. Once cooked, carefully cut the hen in half, garnish with fresh chopped parsley, and serve with the roasted vegetables from Basket 2.

HAZELNUT CHICKEN SALAD WITH STRAWBERRIES

Prep time: **5 minutes** | Cook time: **30 minutes** | Serves **4**

- 2 chicken breasts, cubed
- Salt and pepper to taste
- ¾ cup mayonnaise
- 1 tbsp lime juice
- ½ cup chopped hazelnuts
- ½ cup chopped celery
- ½ cup diced strawberries

1. Sprinkle the cubed chicken breasts with salt and pepper.
2. Preheat the air fryer to 350°F. Place the seasoned chicken cubes in Basket 1 and cook for 9 minutes, shaking halfway through for even cooking. Once done, remove the chicken from the basket and set aside to cool.
3. While the chicken is cooking, place the chopped hazelnuts in Basket 2. Set the air fryer to 350°F and air fry for 3-4 minutes. Once toasted, remove the hazelnuts and set them aside.
4. In a large bowl, combine the cooled chicken, mayonnaise, lime juice, chopped celery, diced strawberries, and toasted hazelnuts. Stir everything together until well combined.
5. Serve the Hazelnut Chicken Salad with Strawberries on a bed of greens or enjoy it as a standalone dish.

TURKEY BURGERS

Prep time: **5 minutes** | Cook time: **13 minutes** | Serves **4**

- 1 pound ground turkey
- ¼ cup diced red onion
- 1 tablespoon grilled chicken seasoning
- ½ teaspoon dried parsley
- ½ teaspoon salt
- 4 slices provolone cheese
- 4 whole-grain sandwich buns
- Suggested toppings: lettuce, sliced tomatoes, dill pickles, and mustard

1. In a large bowl, combine the ground turkey, diced red onion, grilled chicken seasoning, dried parsley, and salt. Mix everything together thoroughly. Shape the mixture into 4 patties.
2. Place the turkey patties in Basket 1 of the air fryer. Cook at 360°F for 11 minutes, or until the turkey is fully cooked and the juices run clear.
3. While the turkey patties cook, split open the sandwich buns and place them in Basket 2. Toast them for 3-4 minutes or until lightly browned. Alternatively, you can toast the buns in Basket 2 while the patties cook in Basket 1.
4. After the 11 minutes are up, top each turkey patty with a slice of provolone cheese. Return the patties to Basket 1 and cook for an additional 2 minutes to melt the cheese.
5. Once the patties are cooked and the cheese is melted, place each turkey patty on a toasted bun. Add your favorite toppings: lettuce, sliced tomatoes, dill pickles, and mustard.
6. Serve the Turkey Burgers with your choice of sides and enjoy a quick, healthy, and delicious meal!

HASSELBACK ALFREDO CHICKEN & ROASTED POTATOES

Prep time: **5 minutes** | Cook time: **20 minutes** |Serves **4**

- 4 boneless, skinless chicken breasts
- 4 teaspoons coconut oil
- ½ teaspoon salt
- ¼ teaspoon ground black pepper
- 4 strips cooked sugar-free bacon,
- broken into 24 pieces
- ½ cup Alfredo sauce
- 1 cup shredded mozzarella cheese
- ¼ teaspoon crushed red pepper flakes

For the second basket:

- 1 cup baby potatoes, halved
- 1 tablespoon olive oil
- ½ teaspoon salt
- ¼ teaspoon ground black pepper

1. Cut six horizontal slits in the top of each chicken breast. Drizzle with coconut oil and sprinkle with salt and black pepper. Place the chicken breasts in one of the air fryer baskets.
2. Place 1 bacon piece in each slit of the chicken breasts. Pour Alfredo sauce over the chicken and sprinkle with mozzarella and crushed red pepper flakes.
3. In the second basket, add the halved baby potatoes. Drizzle with olive oil, then sprinkle with salt and pepper. Toss to coat evenly.
4. Basket 1 (Chicken): Place the chicken into one basket and set the temperature to 370°F.
5. Basket 2 (Potatoes): Place the potatoes in the second basket.
6. Set the timer for 20 minutes, cooking both the chicken and the potatoes simultaneously.
7. The chicken will be done when it reaches an internal temperature of at least 165°F and the cheese is browned. The potatoes should be tender and golden on the outside.
8. Serve the Hasselback Alfredo Chicken with the roasted baby potatoes for a complete meal.

CHICKEN PARMESAN

Prep time: **10 minutes** | Cook time: **20 minutes** |Serves **4**

- 2 chicken breast fillets
- 1 egg, beaten
- ½ cup breadcrumbs
- ¼ cup Parmesan cheese
- 1 tsp Italian seasoning
- 2 tbsp vegetable oil
- 1 cup marinara sauce
- ½ cup shredded mozzarella cheese

1. Dip each fillet in the beaten egg, then coat in a mixture of breadcrumbs, Parmesan, and Italian seasoning.
   Preheat to 350°F.
2. Place one fillet in Basket 1, the other in Basket 2. Air fry at 350°F for 10 minutes, flip, then cook for another 10 minutes.
3. Heat marinara sauce and shred mozzarella while the chicken cooks.
   After 20 minutes, top each chicken fillet with marinara sauce and mozzarella.
4. Return chicken to the air fryer for 3 more minutes at 350°F to melt the cheese.
5. Serve with pasta, salad, or garlic bread.

JERK CHICKEN DRUMSTICKS WITH RICE

Prep time: **10 minutes** | Cook time: **20 minutes** | Serves **2**

- 1 or 2 cloves garlic
- 1 inch of fresh ginger
- 2 serrano peppers (with seeds if you like it spicy, seeds removed for less heat)
- 1 teaspoon ground allspice
- 1 teaspoon ground nutmeg
- 1 teaspoon chili powder
- ½ teaspoon dried thyme
- ½ teaspoon ground cinnamon
- ½ teaspoon paprika
- 1 tablespoon brown sugar
- 1 teaspoon soy sauce
- 2 tablespoons vegetable oil
- 6 skinless chicken drumsticks

For the second basket:
- 1 cup rice
- 1½ cups water or chicken broth (for cooking the rice)

1. Combine all the ingredients except the chicken in a small chopper or blender and blend to a paste. Make slashes into the meat of the chicken drumsticks and rub the spice blend all over the chicken (a pair of plastic gloves makes this really easy). Transfer the rubbed chicken to a non-reactive covered container and let the chicken marinate for at least 30 minutes or overnight in the refrigerator.
2. Preheat the Ninja Foodi 2-Basket Air Fryer to 400°F.
3. Basket 1 (Chicken): Transfer the marinated chicken drumsticks to one of the air fryer baskets.
4. Basket 2 (Rice): Add 1 cup of rice and 1½ cups of water (or chicken broth) to the second basket.
5. Air-fry the chicken for 10 minutes, then turn the drumsticks over and air-fry for another 10 minutes. Meanwhile, the rice will cook in the second basket.
6. Once both the chicken and rice are cooked, serve the jerk chicken with the rice and vegetables or a green salad for a complete meal.

BUFFALO CHICKEN MEATBALLS

Prep time: **5 minutes** | Cook time: **15 minutes** |Serves **4**

- 1 pound ground chicken thighs
- 1 large egg, whisked
- ½ cup hot sauce, divided
- ½ cup crumbled blue cheese
- 2 tablespoons dry ranch seasoning
- ¼ teaspoon salt
- ¼ teaspoon ground black pepper

For the second basket:
- 1 cup celery sticks, cut into 4-inch lengths
- 1 tablespoon olive oil
- ½ teaspoon salt
- ¼ teaspoon black pepper

1. In a large bowl, combine the ground chicken, whisked egg, ¼ cup of hot sauce, blue cheese, ranch seasoning, salt, and pepper. Mix well until fully combined.
2. Divide the mixture into eight equal portions, about ¼ cup each, and form each into a ball.
3. In the second basket, add the celery sticks. Drizzle with olive oil and season with salt and pepper. Toss to coat evenly.
4. Preheat the Ninja Foodi 2-Basket Air Fryer to 370°F.
5. Basket 1 (Meatballs): Place the meatballs into one of the air fryer baskets.
6. Basket 2 (Celery): Place the seasoned celery sticks in the second basket.
7. Set the timer for 15 minutes. After about 7-8 minutes, shake the celery basket to ensure even cooking. Continue cooking until the meatballs are golden and have an internal temperature of at least 165°F.
8. Once the meatballs are done, transfer them to a large serving dish and toss with the remaining ¼ cup hot sauce. Serve with the roasted celery sticks for a complete and tasty meal.

TANGY MUSTARD WINGS WITH SWEET POTATO WEDGES

Prep time: 5 minutes | **Cook time: 25 minutes** | Serves **4**

- 1 pound bone-in chicken wings, separated at joints
- ¼ cup yellow mustard
- ½ teaspoon salt
- ¼ teaspoon ground black pepper

For the second basket:
- 1 cup sweet potato wedges
- 1 tablespoon olive oil
- ½ teaspoon paprika
- ¼ teaspoon sea salt

1. Place the chicken wings in a large bowl and toss with yellow mustard to fully coat. Sprinkle with salt and pepper to season.
2. In the second basket, add the sweet potato wedges. Drizzle with olive oil, then sprinkle with paprika and sea salt. Toss to coat evenly.
3. Preheat the Ninja Foodi 2-Basket Air Fryer to 400°F.
4. Basket 1 (Wings): Place the mustard-coated wings in one of the air fryer baskets.
5. Basket 2 (Sweet Potatoes): Add the seasoned sweet potato wedges to the second basket.
6. Air-fry for 25 minutes, shaking the basket with the wings three times during cooking. At the same time, shake the sweet potato basket once or twice to ensure even cooking.
7. The wings will be done when golden brown and cooked to an internal temperature of at least 165°F. The sweet potatoes should be crispy on the outside and tender on the inside.
8. Once cooked, serve the tangy mustard wings with the sweet potato wedges for a complete meal.

CHAPTER 5: BEEF, LAMB, AND PORK RECIPES

SPICY LAMB CHOPS

Prep time: **15 minutes** | Cook time: **15 minutes** | Serves **4**

- 12 lamb chops, bone-in
- Salt and black pepper, to taste
- ½ teaspoon lemon zest
- 1 tablespoon lemon juice
- 1 teaspoon paprika
- 1 teaspoon garlic powder
- ½ teaspoon Italian seasoning
- ¼ teaspoon onion powder

1. Add the lamb chops to the bowl and sprinkle with salt, garlic powder, Italian seasoning, onion powder, black pepper, lemon zest, lemon juice, and paprika.
2. Rub the chops well, and divide them between both the baskets of the air fryer.
3. Set basket 1 basket to 400 °F, for 15 minutes on AIR FRY mode.
4. Select MATCH for basket 2 basket.
5. After 10 minutes, take out the baskets and flip the chops. Cook for the remaining minutes, and then serve.

BEEF & BROCCOLI

Prep time: **12 minutes** | Cook time: **12 minutes** | Serves **4**

- 12 ounces Teriyaki sauce, divided
- ½ tablespoon garlic powder
- ¼ cup soy sauce
- 1-pound raw sirloin steak, thinly sliced
- 2 cups broccoli, cut into florets
- 2 teaspoons olive oil
- Salt and black pepper, to taste

1. Mix the Teriyaki sauce, salt, garlic powder, black pepper, soy sauce, and olive oil in a zip-lock bag.
2. Add the beef and let it marinate for 2 hours.
3. Drain the beef from the marinade.
4. Toss the broccoli with oil, teriyaki sauce, and salt and black pepper and place in the basket 1 basket.
5. Place the beef in both baskets and set it to SYNC button.
6. Hit START/STOP button and let the cooking cycle complete.
7. Once it's done, take out the beef and broccoli and serve with the leftover Teriyaki sauce and cooked rice.

BBQ BABY PORK RIBS

Prep time: 10 minutes | Cook time: 30 minutes |Serves 6

- 1 rack baby back ribs
- 1 cup BBQ sauce
- 1 cup BBQ rub
- 1 cups water

1. In a bowl, mix together BBQ sauce, BBQ rub and water.
2. Add the pork ribs and coat with the mixture generously.
3. Refrigerate to marinate for about 20 minutes.
4. Grease each basket of "Basket 1" and "Basket 2" of Ninja Foodi 2-Basket Air Fryer.
5. Press "Basket 1" and "Basket 2" and then rotate the knob for each zone to select "Air Fry".
6. Set the temperature to 355 °F for both zones and then set the time for 5 minutes to preheat.
7. After preheating, arrange the ribs into the basket of each zone.
8. Slide each basket into Air Fryer and set the time for 30 minutes.
9. While cooking, flip the ribs once halfway through.
10. After cooking time is completed, remove the ribs from Air Fryer and place onto serving plates.
11. Serve and enjoy!

PORK CHOPS WITH BRUSSELS SPROUTS

Prep time: 15 minutes | Cook time: 15 minutes | Serves 4

- 4 bone-in center-cut pork chop
- Cooking spray
- Salt, to taste
- Black pepper, to taste
- 2 teaspoons olive oil
- 2 teaspoons pure maple syrup
- 2 teaspoons Dijon mustard
- 6 ounces Brussels sprouts, quartered

1. Rub pork chop with salt, ¼ teaspoons black pepper, and cooking spray.
2. Toss Brussels sprouts with mustard, syrup, oil, ¼ teaspoon of black pepper in a medium bowl.
3. Add pork chop to the crisper plate of Basket 1 of the Ninja Foodi 2-Basket Air Fryer.
4. Return the crisper plate to the Ninja Foodi 2-Basket Air Fryer.
5. Choose the Air Fry mode for Basket 1 and set the temperature to 400 °F and the time to 15 minutes.
6. Add the Brussels sprouts to the crisper plate of Basket 2 and return it to the unit.
7. Choose the Air Fry mode for Basket 2 with 350 °F/ 175 degrees C and the time to 13 minutes.
8. Press the SYNC button to sync the finish time for both Zones.
9. Initiate cooking by pressing the START/STOP button.
10. Serve warm and fresh.

SEASONED LAMB STEAK

Prep time: 2 minutes | Cook time: 7 minutes |Serves 2

- 2 lamb steaks
- ½ teaspoon kosher salt
- Drizzle of olive oil
- ½ teaspoon ground black pepper

1. Take a bowl, add every ingredient except lamb steak. Mix well.
2. Rub lamb steaks with a little olive oil.
3. Press each side of steak into salt and pepper mixture.
4. Grease each basket of "Basket 1" and "Basket 2" of Ninja Foodi 2-Basket Air Fryer.
5. Press "Basket 1" and "Basket 2" and then rotate the knob for each zone to select "Air Fry".
6. Set the heat to 400 °F for both zones and then set the time for 5 minutes to preheat.
7. After preheating, arrange steak into the basket of each zone.
8. Slide each basket into Air Fryer and set the time for 5 minutes.
9. While cooking, flip the steak once halfway through and cook for more 5 minutes.
10. After cooking time is completed, remove it from Air Fryer and place onto a platter for about 10 minutes before slicing.
11. With a sharp knife, cut each steak into desired-sized slices and serve.

STEAK FAJITAS WITH ONIONS AND PEPPERS

Prep time: 10 minutes | Cook time: 15 minutes | Serves 6

- 1 pound steak
- 1 green bell pepper, sliced
- 1 yellow bell pepper, sliced
- 1 red bell pepper, sliced
- ½ cup sliced white onions
- 1 packet gluten-free fajita seasoning
- Olive oil spray

1. Thinly slice the steak against the grain. These should be about ¼-inch slices.
2. Mix the steak with the peppers and onions. 3. Evenly coat with the fajita seasoning.
3. Install a crisper plate in both drawers. Place half the steak mixture in the basket 1 drawer and half in basket 2's, then insert the drawers into the unit.
4. Select basket 1, select AIR FRY, set temperature to 390 °F, and set time to 15 minutes. Select MATCH to match basket 2 settings to basket 1. Press the START/STOP button to begin cooking.
5. When the time reaches 10 minutes, press START/STOP to pause the unit. Remove the drawers and flip the steak strips. Re-insert the drawers into the unit and press START/STOP to resume cooking.
6. Serve in warm tortillas.

CHEESESTEAK TAQUITOS

Prep time: **15 minutes** | Cook time: **12 minutes** | Serves **8**

- 1 pack soft corn tortillas
- 136g beef steak strips
- 2 green peppers, sliced
- 1 white onion, chopped
- 1 pkg dry Italian dressing mix
- 10 slices Provolone cheese
- Cooking spray or olive oil

1. Mix beef with cooking oil, peppers, onion, and dressing mix in a bowl.
2. Divide the strips in the air fryer baskets.
3. Return the air fryer basket 1 to Basket 1, and basket 2 to Basket 2 of the Ninja Foodi 2-Basket Air Fryer.
4. Choose the "Air Fry" mode for Basket 1 at 375 °F and 12 minutes of cooking time.
5. Select the "MATCH COOK" option to copy the settings for Basket 2.
6. Initiate cooking by pressing the START/PAUSE BUTTON.
7. Flip the strips once cooked halfway through.
8. Divide the beef strips in the tortillas and top the beef with a beef slice.
9. Roll the tortillas and serve.

LAMB MEATBALLS

Prep time: **10 minutes** | Cook time: **12 minutes** | Serves **8**

- 2 pounds ground lamb
- 4 teaspoons granulated onion
- ½ teaspoon ground cinnamon
- 2 teaspoons ground cumin
- 4 tablespoons fresh parsley
- Salt and black pepper, to taste

1. Add ground lamb, onion, cinnamon, cumin, parsley, salt and pepper in a large bowl. Mix until well combined.
2. Make 1-inch balls from the mixture and set aside.
3. Grease each basket of "Basket 1" and "Basket 2" of Ninja Foodi 2-Basket Air Fryer.
4. Press "Basket 1" and "Basket 2" and then rotate the knob for each zone to select "Air Fry".
5. Set the temperature to 380 °F for both zones and then set the time for 5 minutes to preheat.
6. After preheating, arrange the meatballs into the basket of each zone.
7. Slide each basket into Air Fryer and set the time for 12 minutes.
8. Flip the meatballs once halfway through.
9. Take out and serve warm.

MARINATED STEAK & MUSHROOMS

Prep time: 10 minutes | Cook time: 10 minutes | Serves 4

- 1 lb rib-eye steak, cut into ½-inch pieces
- 2 tsp dark soy sauce
- 2 tsp light soy sauce
- 1 tbsp lime juice
- 1 tbsp rice wine
- 1 tbsp oyster sauce
- 1 tbsp garlic, chopped
- 8 mushrooms, sliced
- 2 tbsp grated ginger
- 1 tsp cornstarch
- ¼ tsp pepper

1. Add steak pieces, mushrooms, and the remaining ingredients to a zip-lock bag. Seal the bag and place it in the refrigerator for 2 hours.
2. Insert a crisper plate in the Ninja Foodi air fryer baskets.
3. Remove the steak pieces and mushrooms from the marinade and place them in both baskets.
4. Select basket 1, then select "air fry" mode and set the temperature to 380 °F for 10 minutes. Press "match" to match basket 2 settings to basket 1. Press "start/stop" to begin. Stir halfway through.

GARLIC SIRLOIN STEAK

Prep time: 10 minutes | Cook time: 10 minutes | Serves 4

- 4 sirloin steaks
- 2 tbsp olive oil
- 2 tbsp steak sauce
- ½ tsp ground coriander
- 1 tsp minced garlic
- 1 tbsp chopped thyme
- Salt, to taste
- Pepper, to taste

1. In a bowl, combine the sirloin steaks with the thyme, olive oil, steak sauce, ground coriander, minced garlic, salt, and pepper. Mix everything well to coat the steaks evenly. Cover and let the steaks marinate for at least 2 hours (or overnight in the fridge for more flavor).
2. Insert the crisper plate into both baskets of your Ninja Foodi 2-Basket Air Fryer. Preheat the air fryer to 360°F.
3. Place two marinated steaks in Basket 1 and the remaining two steaks in Basket 2.
4. Select Basket 1 and set the air fryer to Air Fry mode at 360°F for 10 minutes. Press "Match" and then "Start/Stop" to begin cooking. Both baskets will cook at the same time.
5. After cooking, check that the steaks have reached your desired level of doneness (internal temperature should be at least 145°F for medium-rare). Remove from the baskets and let the steaks rest for 5 minutes before serving.

CHAPTER 6: FISH AND SEAFOOD RECIPES

BREADED SCALLOPS

Prep time: **15 minutes** | **Cook time:** **12 minutes** |**Serves 4**

- ½ cup crushed buttery crackers
- ½ teaspoon garlic powder
- ½ teaspoon seafood seasoning
- 2 tablespoons butter, melted
- 1 pound sea scallops patted dry
- Cooking spray

1. Mix cracker crumbs, garlic powder, and seafood seasoning in a shallow bowl. Spread melted butter in another shallow bowl.
2. Dip each scallop in the melted butter and then roll in the breading to coat well.
3. Grease each Air fryer basket with cooking spray and place half of the scallops in each.
4. Return the crisper plate to the Ninja Foodi 2-Basket Air Fryer.
5. Select the Air Fry mode for Basket 1 and set the temperature to 390 °F and the time to 12 minutes.
6. Press the "MATCH" button to copy the settings for Basket 2.
7. Initiate cooking by pressing the START/STOP button.
8. Flip the scallops with a spatula after 4 minutes and resume cooking.
9. Serve warm.

FISH CAKES

Prep time: **10 minutes** | **Cook time:** **10 minutes** |**Serves 2**

- 6 ounces cod fillets
- ½ cup pork rind panko breadcrumbs
- 1 small egg
- 1 tablespoon mayonnaise
- 1 tablespoon sweet chili sauce
- 1 tablespoon fresh chopped cilantro
- ⅛ teaspoon salt
- ⅛ teaspoon ground black pepper

1. Grease each basket of "Basket 1" and "Basket 2" of Ninja Foodi 2-Basket Air Fryer.
2. Press "Basket 1" and "Basket 2" and then rotate the knob for each zone to select "Air Fry".
3. Set the heat to 400 °F for both zones and then set the time for 5 minutes to preheat.
4. Take a food processor, add cod fillets and process until crumbly.
5. Take a bowl, add crumbled fish, pork rind crumbs, chili sauce, mayo, egg, salt, cilantro and pepper. Stir until well combined.
6. Shape the mixture into patties.
7. After preheating, arrange patties into the basket of each zone.
8. Slide each basket into Air Fryer and set the time for 10 minutes.
9. After cooking time is completed, remove the patties from Air Fryer and serve hot.

CRUSTED TILAPIA

Prep time: 20 minutes | **Cook time: 17 minutes** | **Serves 4**

- ¾ cup breadcrumbs
- 1 packet dry ranch-style dressing
- 2 ½ tablespoons vegetable oil
- 2 eggs beaten
- 4 tilapia fillets
- Herbs and chilies to garnish

1. Thoroughly mix ranch dressing with panko in a bowl.
2. Whisk eggs in a shallow bowl.
3. Dip each fish fillet in the egg, then coat evenly with the panko mixture.
4. Set two coated fillets in each of the crisper plate.
5. Return the crisper plates to the Ninja Foodi 2-Basket Air Fryer.
6. Choose the Air Fry mode for Basket 1 and set the temperature to 390 °F and the time to 17 minutes.
7. Select the "MATCH" button to copy the settings for Basket 2.
8. Initiate cooking by pressing the START/STOP button.
9. Serve warm with herbs and chilies.

GARLIC BUTTER SHRIMP

Prep time: 15 minutes | **Cook time: 8 minutes** |**Serves 6**

- 2 pounds fresh shrimp
- ¾ cup unsalted butter, melted
- 6 tablespoons fresh parsley, chopped
- 4 tablespoons olive oil
- 4 teaspoons minced garlic
- Salt and pepper, to taste

1. Add butter, parsley, olive oil, minced garlic, salt and pepper in a large bowl. Whisk well.
2. Add in shrimp in the mixture and toss to coat well.
3. Press "Basket 1" and "Basket 2" of Ninja Foodi 2-Basket Air Fryer and then rotate the knob for each zone to select "Bake".
4. Set the temperature to 450 °F for both zones and then set the time for 5 minutes to preheat.
5. After preheating, arrange 1 pan into the basket of each zone.
6. Slide each basket into Air Fryer and set the time for 8 minutes.
7. After cooking time is completed, remove the pans from Air Fryer and serve hot.

SMOKED SALMON

Prep time: 20 minutes | **Cook time: 12 minutes** | **Serves 4**

- 2 pounds salmon fillets, smoked
- 6 ounces cream cheese
- 4 tablespoons mayonnaise
- 2 teaspoons chives, fresh
- 1 teaspoon lemon zest
- Salt and freshly ground black pepper, to taste
- 2 tablespoons butter

1. Cut the salmon into very small and uniform bite-size pieces.
2. Mix cream cheese, chives, mayonnaise, black pepper, and lemon zest, in a small mixing bowl.
3. Set it aside for further use.
4. Coat the salmon pieces with salt and butter.
5. Divide the bite-size pieces into both zones of the air fryer.
6. Set it on AIR FRY mode at 400 °F for 12 minutes.
7. Select MATCH for basket 2 basket.
8. Once the salmon is done, top it with the cream cheese mixture and serve.
9. Enjoy hot.

SALMON WITH FENNEL SALAD

Prep time: 10 minutes | **Cook time: 17 minutes** | **Serves 4**

- 2 teaspoons fresh parsley, chopped
- 1 teaspoon fresh thyme, chopped
- 1 teaspoon salt
- 4 (6-oz) skinless center-cut salmon fillets
- 2 tablespoons olive oil
- 4 cups fennel, sliced
- ⅔ cup Greek yogurt
- 1 garlic clove, grated
- 2 tablespoons orange juice
- 1 teaspoon lemon juice
- 2 tablespoons fresh dill, chopped

1. Preheat your Ninja Foodi 2-Basket Air Fryer to 200 °F.
2. Mix ½ teaspoon of salt, thyme, and parsley in a small bowl.
3. Brush the salmon with oil first, then rub liberally rub the herb mixture.
4. Place 2 salmon fillets in each of the crisper plate.
5. Return the crisper plate to the Ninja Foodi 2-Basket Air Fryer.
6. Choose the Air Fry mode for Basket 1 and set the temperature to 390 °F and the time to 17 minutes.
7. Select the "MATCH" button to copy the settings for Basket 2.
8. Initiate cooking by pressing the START/STOP button.
9. Meanwhile, mix fennel with garlic, yogurt, lemon juice, orange juice, remaining salt, and dill in a mixing bowl.
10. Serve the air fried salmon fillets with fennel salad.
11. Enjoy.

SHRIMP WITH LEMON AND PEPPER

Prep time: **5 minutes** | Cook time: **10 minutes** | Serves **4**

- 1-pound medium raw shrimp, peeled and deveined
- ½ cup olive oil
- 2 tablespoons lemon juice
- 1 teaspoon black pepper
- ½ teaspoon salt

1. Place the shrimp in a Ziploc bag with the olive oil, lemon juice, salt, and pepper. Carefully combine all the ingredients.
2. Install a crisper plate in both drawers. Divide the shrimp equally into the two drawers. Insert the drawers into the unit.
3. Select basket 1, then AIR FRY, then set the temperature to 360 °F/ 180 degrees C with a 10-minute timer. To match basket 2 settings to basket 1, choose MATCH. To begin, select START/STOP.
4. Remove the shrimp from the drawers after the timer has finished.

SHRIMP SKEWERS

Prep time: **10minutes** | Cook time: **10 minutes** | Serves **4**

- 1 lb shrimp, peeled and deveined
- 1 tbsp lemon juice
- 1 tbsp olive oil
- 1 tbsp Old Bay seasoning
- 1 tsp minced garlic

1. In a bowl, toss the shrimp with the Old Bay seasoning, minced garlic, lemon juice, and olive oil until the shrimp are evenly coated.
2. Soak wooden skewers in water for about 10 minutes to prevent burning. Then, thread the shrimp onto the soaked skewers.
3. Insert the crisper plate into both baskets of your Ninja Foodi 2-Basket Air Fryer. Preheat the air fryer to 390°F.
4. Place the shrimp skewers in Basket 1 and Basket 2. Select Basket 1, then select Air Fry mode and set the temperature to 390°F for 10 minutes. Press "Match" to match Basket 2 settings to Basket 1. Press "Start/Stop" to begin cooking.
5. Once cooked, check that the shrimp are opaque and slightly golden. Remove the skewers from the baskets and serve warm.

HONEY TERIYAKI TILAPIA

Prep time: **5 minutes** | Cook time: **10 minutes** | Serves **4**

- 8 tablespoons low-sodium teriyaki sauce
- 3 tablespoons honey
- 2 garlic cloves, minced
- 2 tablespoons extra virgin olive oil
- 3 pieces tilapia (each cut into 2 pieces)

1. Combine all the first 4 ingredients to make the marinade.
2. Pour the marinade over the tilapia and let it sit for 20 minutes.
3. Place a crisper plate in each drawer. Place the tilapia in the drawers. Insert the drawers into the unit.
4. Select basket 1, then AIR FRY, then set the temperature to 360 °F with a 10-minute timer. To match basket 2 settings to basket 1, choose MATCH. To begin, select START/STOP.
5. Remove the tilapia from the drawers after the timer has finished.

SPICED TILAPIA

Prep time: **10 minutes** | Cook time: **12 minutes** |Serves **4**

- 1 teaspoon lemon pepper seasoning
- 1 teaspoon garlic powder
- 1 teaspoon onion powder
- Salt and ground black pepper, as required
- 4 (6-ounce) tilapia fillets
- 2 tablespoons olive oil

1. In a small bowl, mix together the spices, salt and black pepper.
2. Coat the tilapia fillets with oil and then rub with spice mixture.
3. Grease each basket of "Basket 1" and "Basket 2" of Ninja Foodi 2-Basket Air Fryer.
4. Press "Basket 1" and "Basket 2" and then rotate the knob for each zone to select "Air Fry".
5. Set the temperature to 360 °F for both zones and then set the time for 5 minutes to preheat.
6. After preheating, arrange 2 tilapia fillets into the basket of each zone.
7. Slide each basket into Air Fryer and set the time for 12 minutes.
8. While cooking, flip the tilapia fillets once halfway through.
9. After cooking time is completed, remove the tilapia fillets and from Air Fryer and serve hot.

SHRIMP SALAD

Prep time: **15 minutes** | Cook time: **5 minutes** | Serves **4**

- 2 romaine hearts, coarsely chopped
- 1 cup cherry tomatoes, halved
- ¼ cup shredded Parmesan cheese
- ½ cup all-purpose flour
- ¾ teaspoon salt
- ½ teaspoon pepper
- 1-pound uncooked shrimp, peeled and deveined
- Cooking spray
- ½ cup Creamy Caesar Salad Dressing

1. Combine romaine hearts, tomatoes, and cheese in a large mixing basin; chill until ready to serve.
2. Combine flour, salt, and pepper in a small bowl. Toss in a few pieces of shrimp at a time, tossing to coat; brush off excess.
3. Press "Basket 1" and "Basket 2" and then rotate the knob for each zone to select "Air Fry".
4. Set the temperature to 375 °F for both zones, and then set the time for 5 minutes to preheat.
5. After preheating, spray the Air-Fryer basket of each zone with cooking spray, arrange shrimp in a single layer, and spritz them with cooking spray.
6. Slide the basket into Air Fryer and set the time for 4 minutes.
7. Carefully turn them and cook 4 minutes longer.
8. After cooking time is completed, toss the romaine mixture with the dressing to coat it, put shrimps on top, and place them on a serving plate and serve.

CRISPY FISH NUGGETS

Prep time: **10 minutes** | Cook time: **8 minutes** | Serves **4**

- 2 large eggs
- ¾ cup all-purpose flour
- 1 ½ lbs cod fish fillets, cut into bite-sized pieces
- 1 tsp garlic powder
- 1 tbsp Old Bay seasoning
- Salt and pepper, to taste

1. In a small bowl, whisk the eggs until smooth.
2. In a shallow dish, combine the flour, garlic powder, Old Bay seasoning, salt, and pepper.
3. Dip each piece of fish into the flour mixture, then into the beaten eggs, and coat it again in the flour mixture for a crispy finish.
4. Insert the crisper plate into both baskets of your Ninja Foodi 2-Basket Air Fryer. Preheat the air fryer to 380°F.
5. Place the coated fish pieces evenly in both baskets. Select Basket 1, then choose Air Fry mode and set the temperature to 380°F for 8 minutes. Press "Match" to sync Basket 2 with Basket 1 settings. Press "Start/Stop" to begin cooking.
6. Once the fish nuggets are golden and crispy, remove them from the baskets. Serve warm with your favourite dipping sauce.

CHILI LIME TILAPIA

Prep time: **15 minutes** | Cook time: **10 minutes** | Serves **4**

- ¾ lb tilapia fillets
- 2 tsp chili powder
- 1 tsp cumin
- 1 tsp garlic powder
- ½ tsp oregano
- ½ tsp sea salt
- ¼ tsp black pepper
- Zest of 1 lime
- Juice of ½ lime

1. In a bowl, combine the chili powder, cumin, garlic powder, oregano, salt, pepper, lime zest, and lime juice.
2. Rub the spice mixture evenly over both sides of the tilapia fillets.
3. Place two fillets in each air fryer basket. Insert the baskets into the Ninja Foodi 2-Basket Air Fryer.
4. Select Basket 1, choose Air Fry mode, set the temperature to 400°F, and cook for 10 minutes.
5. Press "Match Cook" to copy the settings to Basket 2.
6. Press the Start/Pause button to begin cooking.
7. Halfway through the cooking time, flip the tilapia fillets to ensure even cooking.
8. Once the tilapia is cooked through and crispy, remove from the air fryer and serve warm.

SCALLOPS WITH GREENS

Prep time: **15 minutes** | Cook time: **13 minutes** | Serves **8**

- ¾ cup heavy whipping cream
- 1 tablespoon tomato paste
- 1 tablespoon chopped fresh basil
- 1 teaspoon garlic, minced
- ½ teaspoons salt
- ½ teaspoons pepper
- 12 ounces frozen spinach thawed
- 8 jumbo sea scallops
- Vegetable oil to spray

1. Season the scallops with vegetable oil, salt, and pepper in a bowl
2. Mix cream with spinach, basil, garlic, salt, pepper, and tomato paste in a bowl.
3. Pour this mixture over the scallops and mix gently.
4. Divide the scallops in the Air Fryers Baskets without using the crisper plate.
5. Return the crisper plate to the Ninja Foodi 2-Basket Air Fryer.
6. Choose the Air Fry mode for Basket 1 and set the temperature to 390 °F and the time to 13 minutes.
7. Select the "MATCH" button to copy the settings for Basket 2.
8. Initiate cooking by pressing the START/STOP button.
9. Serve right away.

CHAPTER 7:
VEGETABLES AND
SIDES RECIPES

FRIED OLIVES

Prep time: 15 minutes | Cook time: 9 minutes |Serves 6

- 2 cups blue cheese stuffed olives, drained
- ½ cup all-purpose flour
- 1 cup panko breadcrumbs
- ½ teaspoon garlic powder
- 1 pinch oregano
- 2 eggs

1. Mix flour with oregano and garlic powder in a bowl and beat two eggs in another bowl.
2. Spread panko breadcrumbs in a bowl.
3. Coat all the olives with the flour mixture, dip in the eggs and then coat with the panko breadcrumbs.
4. As you coat the olives, place them in the two crisper plates in a single layer, then spray them with cooking oil.
5. Return the crisper plates to the Ninja Foodi 2-Basket Air Fryer.
6. Choose the Air Fry mode for Basket 1 and set the temperature to 375 °F and the time to 9 minutes.
7. Select the "MATCH" button to copy the settings for Basket 2.
8. Initiate cooking by pressing the START/STOP button.
9. Flip the olives once cooked halfway through, then resume cooking.
10. Serve.

LIME GLAZED TOFU

Prep time: 10 minutes | Cook time: 14 minutes |Serves 6

- ⅔ cup coconut aminos
- 2 (14-oz) packages extra-firm, water-packed tofu, drained
- 6 tablespoons toasted sesame oil
- ⅔ cup lime juice
- 2 tablespoons sesame seeds (for garnish)

1. Pat dry the tofu bars with paper towels and slice into half-inch cubes.
2. Toss the coconut aminos, toasted sesame oil, lime juice, and sesame seeds in a small bowl.
3. Marinate the tofu cubes in the mixture for 4 hours in the refrigerator. Drain off any excess marinade and water before cooking.
4. Divide the marinated tofu cubes between the two crisper plates.
5. Return the crisper plates to the Ninja Foodi 2-Basket Air Fryer.
6. Choose the Air Fry mode for Basket 1 and set the temperature to 400°F with a cook time of 14 minutes.
7. Select the MATCH button to copy the settings for Basket 2.
8. Press START/STOP to begin cooking.
9. Toss the tofu halfway through the cooking process, then resume cooking.
10. Once done, sprinkle additional sesame seeds on top and serve warm.

LEMON BUTTER GREEN BEANS WITH GARLIC HERB ROASTED POTATOES

Prep time: **10 minutes** | Cook time: **15 minutes** |Serves **6**

For the Lemon Butter Green Beans (Basket 1):

- 1 lb. green beans, sliced
- 2 tablespoons olive oil
- 2 cloves garlic, minced
- 2 tablespoons lemon juice
- 1 tablespoon Parmesan cheese
- 2 tablespoons butter

For the Garlic Herb Roasted Potatoes (Basket 2):

- 2 medium potatoes, diced
- 1 tablespoon olive oil
- 1 teaspoon dried rosemary
- 1 teaspoon garlic powder
- Salt and pepper, to taste

1. Toss the sliced green beans with 2 tablespoons of olive oil.
2. Place the green beans in Basket 1 of the air fryer.
3. Dice the potatoes and toss them in olive oil, dried rosemary, garlic powder, salt, and pepper.
4. Place the potatoes in Basket 2.
5. Select the air fry setting and cook the green beans at 390°F for 10 minutes, stirring once or twice halfway through to ensure even cooking.
6. Air fry the potatoes at 390°F for 12–15 minutes, shaking the basket halfway through, until they are golden and crispy.
7. While the green beans and potatoes are cooking, melt 2 tablespoons of butter in a small pan over medium heat.
8. Add the minced garlic and cook for 30 seconds, then stir in the lemon juice and Parmesan cheese. Cook for 1 more minute and remove from heat.
9. Once the green beans are done, pour the lemon butter sauce over them and toss to coat evenly.
10. Serve the Lemon Butter Green Beans alongside the Garlic Herb Roasted Potatoes for a delicious, well-rounded meal.

MINI HASSELBACK POTATOES WITH GARLIC GREEN BEANS

Prep time: 5 minutes | Cook time: 25 minutes | Serves 4

For the Mini Hasselback Potatoes:

- 1½ pounds baby Yukon Gold potatoes (about 10)
- 5 tablespoons butter, cut into very thin slices
- Salt and freshly ground black pepper
- 1 tablespoon vegetable oil
- ¼ cup grated Parmesan cheese (optional)
- Chopped fresh parsley or chives

For the Garlic Green Beans:

- 12 ounces fresh green beans, trimmed
- 1 tablespoon olive oil
- 2 garlic cloves, minced
- Salt and pepper, to taste

1. Make six to eight deep vertical slits across the top of each potato about three-quarters of the way down. Ensure the slits are deep enough to allow the slices to spread apart but don't cut all the way through the potato. Place a thin slice of butter between each of the slits and season generously with salt and pepper.
2. In a bowl, toss the green beans with olive oil, minced garlic, salt, and pepper until well coated.
3. Place the potatoes in one basket of the Ninja Foodi 2-Basket Air Fryer, packing them in next to each other. It's fine if some of the potatoes sit on top of one another.
4. Add the garlic green beans to the second basket, arranging them in a single layer.
5. Air-fry both baskets at 400°F for 20 minutes. Shake the green beans halfway through for even cooking.
6. After 20 minutes, spray or brush the potatoes with a little vegetable oil, and sprinkle the Parmesan cheese on top. Continue to air-fry the potatoes for an additional 5 minutes. Meanwhile, give the green beans a stir.
7. Once the potatoes are crispy and golden, and the green beans are tender and slightly browned, remove both baskets from the air fryer.
8. Garnish the potatoes with chopped parsley or chives, and serve them hot alongside the garlic green beans.

DOUBLE CHEESE-BROCCOLI TOTS WITH ROASTED GARLIC MUSHROOMS

Prep time: **5 minutes** | Cook time: **30 minutes** | Serves **4**

For the Double Cheese-Broccoli Tots (Basket 1):

- ⅓ cup grated sharp cheddar cheese
- 1 cup riced broccoli
- 1 egg
- 1 oz herbed Boursin cheese
- 1 tbsp grated onion
- ⅓ cup bread crumbs
- ½ tsp salt
- ¼ tsp garlic powder

For the Roasted Garlic Mushrooms (Basket 2):

- 8 oz button mushrooms, sliced
- 1 tablespoon olive oil
- 2 cloves garlic, minced
- Salt and pepper, to taste

1. Preheat the air fryer to 375°F.
2. In a bowl, mix the riced broccoli, egg, cheddar cheese, Boursin cheese, grated onion, bread crumbs, salt, and garlic powder.
3. Form the mixture into 12 rectangular mounds (tots).
4. Slice the mushrooms and place them in a bowl.
5. Drizzle with olive oil, add the minced garlic, and season with salt and pepper. Toss to coat evenly.
6. Cut a piece of parchment paper to fit the bottom of Basket 1.
7. Place the broccoli tots on the parchment paper in a single layer. Air-fry for 9 minutes at 375°F, flipping halfway through.
8. While the tots are cooking, place the seasoned mushrooms in Basket 2.
9. Air-fry at 375°F for 8–10 minutes, stirring halfway through, until golden and tender.
10. Once both the Double Cheese-Broccoli Tots and Roasted Garlic Mushrooms are cooked, remove them from the air fryer.
11. Let the tots chill for 5 minutes before serving.

PESTO VEGETABLE SKEWERS WITH CRISPY SWEET POTATO WEDGES

Prep time: 5 minutes | Cook time: 8 minutes | Serves 8

For the Pesto Vegetable Skewers (Basket 1):
- 1 medium zucchini, trimmed and cut into ½" slices
- ½ medium yellow onion, peeled and cut into 1» squares
- 1 medium red bell pepper, seeded and cut into 1" squares
- 16 whole cremini mushrooms
- ⅓ cup basil pesto
- ½ teaspoon salt
- ¼ teaspoon ground black pepper

For the Crispy Sweet Potato Wedges (Basket 2):
- 2 medium sweet potatoes, cut into wedges
- 1 tablespoon olive oil
- 1 teaspoon paprika
- Salt and pepper, to taste

1. Preheat the air fryer to 375°F.
2. Divide zucchini slices, onion, and bell pepper into eight even portions.
3. Thread onto 6" skewers, alternating the vegetables and adding 2 mushrooms to each skewer.
4. Brush each kebab generously with basil pesto and sprinkle with salt and pepper on all sides.
5. Cut the sweet potatoes into wedges.
6. Toss the wedges in olive oil, paprika, salt, and pepper.
7. Place the skewers in Basket 1 and air-fry for 8 minutes, turning halfway through, until the vegetables are browned at the edges and tender-crisp
8. Place the sweet potato wedges in Basket 2 and air-fry for 10–12 minutes at 375°F, shaking the basket halfway through, until golden and crispy.
9. Once both the Pesto Vegetable Skewers and Crispy Sweet Potato Wedges are cooked, remove from the air fryer.
10. Serve the skewers warm alongside the crispy sweet potato wedges for a full meal.

SRIRACHA GREEN BEANS WITH CRISPY TOFU BITES

Prep time: **5 minutes** | Cook time: **30 minutes** | Serves **4**

For the Sriracha Green Beans (Basket 1):
- 12 oz trimmed green beans
- 1 tbsp tamari
- ½ tbsp Sriracha sauce
- 4 tsp canola oil
- ½ tbsp toasted sesame seeds
- 1 tbsp cilantro, chopped

For the Crispy Tofu Bites (Basket 2):
- 1 block firm tofu, drained and cubed
- 1 tablespoon olive oil
- 1 tablespoon soy sauce
- 1 teaspoon cornstarch
- 1 tsp garlic powder
- Salt and pepper, to taste

1. Preheat the air fryer to 375°F.
2. In a small bowl, mix the tamari, Sriracha sauce, and 1 tsp of canola oil. Set aside.
3. In a large bowl, toss the green beans with the remaining canola oil, coating them evenly.
4. Drain the tofu and cut it into bite-sized cubes.
5. In a bowl, toss the tofu cubes with olive oil, soy sauce, cornstarch, garlic powder, salt, and pepper until well-coated.
6. Place the green beans in Basket 1 of the air fryer and air-fry for 8 minutes, shaking the basket once halfway through, until the beans are charred and tender.
7. While the green beans cook, place the tofu cubes in Basket 2.
8. Air-fry for 10–12 minutes at 375°F, shaking the basket halfway through, until crispy and golden brown.
9. Once the green beans are done, toss them with the Sriracha sauce, cilantro, and toasted sesame seeds.
10. Serve the Sriracha Green Beans with Crispy Tofu Bites for a delicious and satisfying meal!

BEET FRIES WITH ROASTED BROCCOLI

Prep time: 5 minutes | Cook time: 22 minutes | Serves 3

For the Beet Fries
- 3 6-ounce red beets
- Vegetable oil spray
- Coarse sea salt or kosher salt (to taste)

For the Roasted Broccoli
- 1 small head of broccoli, cut into florets
- 1 tablespoon olive oil
- Salt and pepper (to taste)

1. Preheat the air fryer to 375°F.
2. Remove the stems from the beets and peel them with a knife or vegetable peeler. Slice them into ½-inch-thick circles. Lay these flat on a cutting board and slice them into ½-inch-thick sticks. Generously coat the sticks on all sides with vegetable oil spray.
3. In a bowl, toss the broccoli florets with olive oil, salt, and pepper until evenly coated.
4. Place the beet fries into one basket of the air fryer, ensuring they are spread out evenly.
5. In the second basket, add the broccoli florets, spreading them out in a single layer.
6. Air-fry both baskets at 375°F for 22 minutes. Shake the beet fries every 5 minutes to ensure even cooking. Stir the broccoli halfway through for even roasting. If your air fryer is set at 360°F, add an extra 2 minutes to the cooking time.
7. Once the beet fries are browned and crisp at the ends, and the broccoli is tender and slightly browned, remove both baskets from the air fryer.
8. Pour the beet fries into a large bowl, add the coarse sea salt, and toss well. Serve the fries alongside the roasted broccoli.

TOMATO & SQUASH STUFFED MUSHROOMS WITH GARLIC ROASTED BABY CARROTS

Prep time: **5 minutes** | Cook time: **15 minutes** | Serves **2**

For the Tomato & Squash Stuffed Mushrooms (Basket 1):
- 12 whole white button mushrooms
- 3 tsp olive oil
- 2 tbsp diced zucchini
- 1 tsp soy sauce
- ¼ tsp salt
- 2 tbsp tomato paste
- 1 tbsp chopped parsley

For the Garlic Roasted Baby Carrots (Basket 2):
- 10–12 baby carrots, peeled
- 1 tablespoon olive oil
- 1 clove garlic, minced
- Salt and pepper, to taste

1. Preheat the air fryer to 350°F.
2. Remove the stems from the mushrooms and finely chop them. Set aside in a bowl.
3. Brush 1 tsp of olive oil around the top ridge of the mushroom caps.
4. Add the chopped mushroom stems, diced zucchini, soy sauce, salt, and tomato paste to the bowl and mix well.
5. Toss the baby carrots in olive oil, minced garlic, salt, and pepper.
6. Divide the mixture evenly and press it into the tops of the mushroom caps.
7. Place the stuffed mushrooms in Basket 1 of the air fryer and air-fry for 5 minutes, until the mushrooms are tender.
8. While the mushrooms are cooking, place the seasoned baby carrots in Basket 2.
9. Air-fry for 10 minutes at 350°F, shaking the basket halfway through.
10. Once both the stuffed mushrooms and garlic roasted carrots are cooked, remove them from the air fryer.
11. Garnish the Mushrooms with chopped parsley and serve alongside the roasted carrots.

CHAPTER 8: DESSERTS AND SWEETS

AMARETTO CHEESECAKE

Prep time: 5 minutes | Cook time: 35 minutes | Serves 6

- ⅔ cup slivered almonds
- ½ cup Corn Chex
- 1 tbsp light brown sugar
- 3 tbsp butter, melted
- 14 oz cream cheese
- 2 tbsp sour cream
- ½ cup granulated sugar
- ½ cup Amaretto liqueur
- ½ tsp lemon juice
- 2 tbsp almond flakes

1. In a food processor, pulse the Corn Chex, slivered almonds, and brown sugar until a fine powder forms.
2. Transfer to a bowl and stir in the melted butter. Mix until the butter is evenly distributed.
3. Press this crust mixture into the base of a greased springform pan.
4. In a separate bowl, combine the cream cheese, sour cream, granulated sugar, Amaretto liqueur, and lemon juice. Stir until smooth.
5. Pour the cheesecake filling over the prepared crust in the springform pan.
6. Preheat Basket 1 of the air fryer to 400°F for 3 minutes.
7. Once preheated, place the springform pan into Basket 1.
8. Cover the cheesecake with aluminum foil to prevent over-browning.
9. Set the timer for 16 minutes.
10. While Basket 1 is cooking, place the slivered almonds in Basket 2.
11. Air fry the almonds at 350°F for 5 minutes, shaking the basket halfway through to ensure even browning.
12. Once done, set aside.
13. After 16 minutes, remove the foil from the cheesecake in Basket 1.
14. Cook for another 6 minutes, or until the cheesecake is firm with a slight jiggle in the center.
15. Once cooking is complete, remove the cheesecake from Basket 1. Allow it to cool at room temperature.
16. Place it in the fridge for at least 2 hours to fully set.
17. Once the cheesecake has chilled, release the sides of the springform pan.
18. Top the cheesecake with the toasted almonds from Basket 2 and serve.

FRIED PINEAPPLE CHUNKS

Prep time: 5 minutes | Cook time: 10 minutes | Serves 4

- 3 tablespoons cornstarch
- 1 large egg white, beaten until foamy
- 1 cup ground vanilla wafer cookies (not low-fat cookies)
- ¼ teaspoon ground dried ginger
- 18 fresh 1-inch chunks peeled and cored pineapple

1. Preheat both Basket 1 and Basket 2 to 400°F for 5 minutes.
2. In a medium or large bowl, place the cornstarch.
3. In a separate small bowl, beat the egg white until foamy.
4. In a large zip-closed plastic bag, combine the ground vanilla wafer cookies and ground dried ginger. Shake gently to mix.
5. Dump the pineapple chunks into the bowl with the cornstarch. Toss and stir until the pineapple is well coated.
6. Working in batches, dip the cornstarch-coated pineapple chunks into the egg white, then transfer them into the bag with the cookie mixture. Seal the bag and shake gently to coat each piece evenly.
7. Divide the coated pineapple chunks between Basket 1 and Basket 2, ensuring they don't touch and there's space for air circulation.
8. Air-fry undisturbed for 10 minutes, or until golden brown and crispy. Check halfway through for even cooking.
9. Once cooked, gently transfer the pineapple chunks to a wire rack to cool for at least 5 minutes (or up to 15 minutes) before serving. This will help them crisp up further.
10. Serve warm and enjoy your delicious fried pineapple chunks!

CITRUS MOUSSE

Prep time: 10 minutes | Cook time: 12 minutes |Serves 4

- 8 ounces cream cheese, softened
- 1 cup heavy cream
- 4 tablespoons fresh lime juice
- 4 tablespoons maple syrup
- Pinch of salt

1. For mousse: Press "Basket 1" and "Basket 2" and then rotate the knob for each zone to select "Bake".
2. Set the temperature to 350 °F for both zones and then set the time for 5 minutes to preheat.
3. In a bowl, add all the ingredients and mix until well combined.
4. Transfer the mixture into 4 ramekins.
5. After preheating, arrange 2 ramekins into the basket of each zone.
6. Slide each basket into Air Fryer and set the time for 12 minutes.
7. After cooking time is completed, remove the ramekins from Air Fryer.
8. Set the ramekins aside to cool.
9. Refrigerate the ramekins for at least 3 hours before serving.

APPLE CRUMBLE

Prep time: 5 minutes | Cook time: 25 minutes |Serves 4

- 1 can apple pie filling
- 6 tablespoons caster sugar
- 8 tablespoons self-rising flour
- ¼ cup butter, softened
- A pinch of salt

1. Divide the apple pie filling evenly between two small baking dishes (one for each basket). Spread the apple filling out in each dish so it covers the base.
2. In a large bowl, combine the caster sugar, self-rising flour, butter, and a pinch of salt. Mix well until the mixture forms a crumbly texture.
3. Evenly distribute the crumble mixture over the apple pie filling in both baking dishes. Press down slightly to compact the topping.
4. Preheat both baskets in the air fryer by selecting "Bake" mode on both Basket 1 and Basket 2. Set the temperature to 320°F and the preheat time for 5 minutes.
5. Once preheated, place one baking dish in Basket 1 and the other in Basket 2.
6. Set the cooking time for 25 minutes.
7. Once the cooking time is complete, carefully remove both dishes from the air fryer.
8. Set aside to cool slightly.
9. Serve and enjoy!

PUMPKIN PIE

Prep time: **5 minutes** | Cook time: **25 minutes** |Serves **6**

- 1 can pumpkin pie mix
- 1 large egg
- 1 teaspoon vanilla extract
- ⅓ cup sweetened condensed milk
- 1 premade graham cracker piecrust

1. In a large bowl, whisk together the pumpkin pie mix, egg, vanilla extract, and sweetened condensed milk until well combined.
2. Pour the mixture into the premade graham cracker piecrusts. If you have two pies, use two premade piecrusts.
3. Preheat both Basket 1 and Basket 2 to 325°F for 5 minutes.
4. Place one pie in Basket 1 and the other in Basket 2.
5. Set the timer for 25 minutes, checking halfway through for even cooking. Both pies should become golden and firm, and a toothpick inserted into the center of each should come out clean.
6. Once the pies are cooked, remove from the air fryer and let them cool to room temperature.
7. Chill in the refrigerator for at least 2 hours until fully set.
8. Slice and enjoy your perfectly cooked pumpkin pies!

CHOCOLATE DOUGHNUT HOLES

Prep time: **5 minutes** | Cook time: **6 minutes** |Serves **20**

- 1 cup blanched finely ground almond flour
- ½ cup low-carb vanilla protein powder
- ½ cup granular erythritol
- ¼ cup unsweetened cocoa powder
- ½ teaspoon baking powder
- 2 large eggs, whisked
- ½ teaspoon vanilla extract

1. In a large bowl, mix all ingredients until a soft dough forms.
2. Roll the dough into twenty balls, about 2 tablespoons each.
3. Cut two pieces of parchment paper to fit the bottom of both baskets.
4. Place the doughnut holes into the baskets, ensuring they are not overcrowded and have space around them for air circulation.
5. Preheat both baskets by selecting Air Fry mode on both Basket 1 and Basket 2. Set the temperature to 380°F for both baskets and preheat for 5 minutes.
6. Once preheated, place half of the doughnut holes in Basket 1 and the remaining doughnut holes in Basket 2.
7. Set the timer for 6 minutes, flipping the doughnut holes halfway through cooking for even crispiness.
8. After cooking, allow the doughnut holes to cool completely for about 10 minutes.
9. Serve and enjoy your delicious, low-carb chocolate doughnut holes!

CHERRY HAND PIES

Prep time: **5 minutes** | Cook time: **8 minutes** | Serves **8**

- 4 cups frozen or canned pitted tart cherries (if using canned, drain and pat dry)
- 2 teaspoons lemon juice
- ½ cup sugar
- ¼ cup cornstarch
- 1 teaspoon vanilla extract
- 1 Basic Pie Dough (or store-bought pie dough)

1. In a medium saucepan, place the cherries and lemon juice. Cook over medium heat for 10 minutes or until the cherries begin to break down.
2. In a small bowl, stir together the sugar and cornstarch. Add the mixture to the cherries, stirring constantly. Cook over low heat for 2-3 minutes until thickened. Remove from the heat and stir in the vanilla extract. Allow the cherry mixture to cool to room temperature (about 30 minutes).
3. Bring the pie dough to room temperature. Divide the dough into 8 equal pieces. Roll out each piece to ¼-inch thickness in circles. Place ¼ cup filling in the center of each circle. Fold the dough over to create a half-circle. Use a fork to press the edges together to seal the pies and pierce the top for steam release.
4. Preheat both Basket 1 and Basket 2 to 350°F for 3 minutes.
5. Place a single layer of hand pies in Basket 1 (or both baskets if you want to cook more than 4 at a time). Spray lightly with cooking spray. Air-fry for 8 to 10 minutes, or until golden brown and cooked through.

KIWI PASTRY BITES

Prep time: **5 minutes** | Cook time: **45 minutes** |Serves **6**

- 3 kiwi fruits, cut into 12 pieces
- 12 wonton wrappers
- ½ cup peanut butter

1. Lay out the wonton wrappers on a flat, clean surface.
2. Place one piece of kiwi on each wrapper and add 1 teaspoon of peanut butter on top.
3. Fold each wrapper from one corner to another to create a triangle.
4. Bring the two bottom corners together, but do not seal completely. Gently press out any air, then press the open edges to seal the wonton bites.
5. Preheat both Basket 1 and Basket 2 to 370°F for 5 minutes. You can lightly grease the baskets or use parchment paper if needed to prevent sticking.
6. Place 6 wontons in Basket 1 and the remaining 6 wontons in Basket 2.
7. Set the timer for 15-18 minutes, flipping the wontons halfway through cooking to ensure they become golden and crisp.
8. Keep an eye on the progress for even browning.
9. Once the wontons are golden and crispy, remove from the baskets and let cool for a few minutes before serving.
10. Serve and enjoy these crispy kiwi pastry bites with a touch of peanut butter!

WHITE CHOCOLATE CRANBERRY BLONDIES

Prep time: 5 minutes | **Cook time: 18 minutes** | **Serves 6**

- ⅓ cup butter
- ½ cup sugar
- 1 teaspoon vanilla extract
- 1 large egg
- 1 cup all-purpose flour
- ½ teaspoon baking powder
- ⅛ teaspoon salt
- ¼ cup dried cranberries
- ¼ cup white chocolate chips

1. Preheat both Basket 1 and Basket 2 to 320°F for 3 minutes.
2. In a large bowl, cream the butter with the sugar and vanilla extract until smooth.
3. Whisk in the egg and set aside.
4. In a separate bowl, combine flour, baking powder, and salt. Gently fold the dry ingredients into the wet mixture.
5. Fold in the dried cranberries and white chocolate chips.
6. Liberally spray an oven-safe 7-inch springform pan with olive oil. Pour the prepared batter into the pan, spreading evenly.
7. Place the springform pan in Basket 1 and set the air fryer to 17 minutes at 320°F.
8. Check for doneness by inserting a toothpick into the center. If it comes out clean, the blondies are done.
9. If you want to toast extra cranberries or white chocolate chips, place them in Basket 2 for 2-3 minutes at 320°F to toast lightly, then sprinkle them over the top of the blondies after they're done baking.
10. Let the blondies cool for 5 minutes before removing them from the pan.
11. Slice and serve warm!

BLUEBERRY CRISP

Prep time: **5 minutes** | Cook time: **18 minutes** | Serves **6**

- 2 cups fresh blueberries
- ½ cup granulated sugar
- 2 tablespoons instant tapioca
- ½ cup all-purpose flour
- ½ cup rolled oats
- ¼ cup chopped nuts (optional)
- ¼ cup brown sugar
- 4 tablespoons butter, cubed
- 1 teaspoon ground cinnamon
- ½ teaspoon salt

1. Preheat both Basket 1 and Basket 2 to 400°F for 3 minutes.
2. In a 6-inch round cake pan (for small batch), 7-inch round cake pan (for medium batch), or 8-inch round cake pan (for large batch), mix the blueberries, granulated sugar, and instant tapioca.
3. While the air fryer is preheating, prepare the topping: In a medium bowl, combine flour, oats, nuts (if using), brown sugar, butter, cinnamon, and salt. Mix until the mixture forms a crumbly texture.
4. Once both baskets are preheated, place the cake pan with the blueberry mixture into Basket 1. Air-fry for 5 minutes or until the blueberries begin to bubble.
5. While the blueberries cook in Basket 1, place the topping mixture evenly onto a sheet of parchment paper or a separate pan in Basket 2. Air-fry for 5 minutes to toast the topping ingredients.
6. Once the blueberries in Basket 1 begin to bubble, crumble the toasted topping mixture evenly over the blueberries.
7. Return the pan to Basket 1 and continue air-frying undisturbed for 8 minutes, or until the topping has browned and the filling is bubbling.
8. Carefully remove the cake pan from Basket 1 using hot pads or silicone mitts.
9. Let the crisp cool for at least 10 minutes, or to room temperature, before serving.

AIR FRY BROWNIES

Prep time: **20 minutes** | Cook time: **35 minutes** |Serves **2**

- ¼ cup butter, melted
- ½ cup sugar
- 1 egg
- ½ teaspoon vanilla extract
- ⅓ cup all-purpose flour
- 3 tablespoons unsweetened cocoa
- ⅛ teaspoon baking powder
- ⅛ teaspoon salt

1. Combine melted butter and sugar in a medium mixing bowl. Mix in the egg and vanilla extract thoroughly.
2. Stir in the dry ingredients until barely mixed.
3. Pour batter into the pans that have been prepared.
4. Press "Basket 1" and "Basket 2" and then rotate the knob for each zone to select "Air Fryer".
5. Set the temperature to 330 °F for both zones, and then set the time for 5 minutes to preheat.
6. After preheating, place pans into the Air Fryer basket of each zone.
7. Slide the baskets into Air Fryer and set the time for 13 minutes.
8. After cooking time is completed, transfer onto serving plates and serve.

SWEET BITES

Prep time: **25 minutes** | Cook time: **12 minutes** | Serves **4**

- 10 sheets Phyllo dough (filo dough)
- 2 tablespoons melted butter
- 1 cup walnuts, chopped
- 2 teaspoons honey
- 1 pinch of cinnamon
- 1 teaspoon orange zest
- ½ cup fresh blueberries

1. First, layer together 10 sheets of Phyllo dough on a flat surface.
2. Cut the dough into 4 x 4-inch squares.
3. Coat the squares with melted butter, then drizzle honey over them. Sprinkle with orange zest, walnuts, cinnamon, and a few fresh blueberries.
4. Bring all 4 corners of each square together and press them to create a little purse-like design, making sure to seal the edges tightly.
5. Divide the filled phyllo purses evenly between both air fryer baskets.
6. Select Basket 1 and set the air fryer to AIR FRY mode at 375°F for 7 minutes.
7. Select the MATCH button for Basket 2 to sync the settings.
8. Once done, carefully remove the sweet bites from the air fryer and serve warm.

MEASUREMENT CONVERSION CHART

VOLUME EQUIVALENTS(DRY)

US STANDARD	METRIC (APPROXIMATE)
1/8 teaspoon	0.5 mL
1/4 teaspoon	1 mL
1/2 teaspoon	2 mL
3/4 teaspoon	4 mL
1 teaspoon	5 mL
1 tablespoon	15 mL
1/4 cup	59 mL
1/2 cup	118 mL
3/4 cup	177 mL
1 cup	235 mL
2 cups	475 mL
3 cups	700 mL
4 cups	1 L

VOLUME EQUIVALENTS(LIQUID)

US STANDARD	US STANDARD (OUNCES)	METRIC (APPROXIMATE)
2 tablespoons	1 fl.oz.	30 mL
1/4 cup	2 fl.oz.	60 mL
1/2 cup	4 fl.oz.	120 mL
1 cup	8 fl.oz.	240 mL
1 1/2 cup	12 fl.oz.	355 mL
2 cups or 1 pint	16 fl.oz.	475 mL
4 cups or 1 quart	32 fl.oz.	1 L
1 gallon	128 fl.oz.	4 L

TEMPERATURES EQUIVALENTS

FAHRENHEIT(F)	CELSIUS(C) (APPROXIMATE)
225 °F	107 °C
250 °F	120 °C
275 °F	135 °C
300 °F	150 °C
325 °F	160 °C
350 °F	180 °C
375 °F	190 °C
400 °F	205 °C
425 °F	220 °C
450 °F	235 °C
475 °F	245 °C
500 °F	260 °C

WEIGHT EQUIVALENTS

US STANDARD	METRIC (APPROXIMATE)
1 ounce	28 g
2 ounces	57 g
5 ounces	142 g
10 ounces	284 g
15 ounces	425 g
16 ounces (1 pound)	455 g
1.5 pounds	680 g
2 pounds	907 g

The Dirty Dozen and Clean Fifteen

The Environmental Working Group (EWG) is a nonprofit, nonpartisan organization dedicated to protecting human health and the environment Its mission is to empower people to live healthier lives in a healthier environment. This organization publishes an annual list of the twelve kinds of produce, in sequence, that have the highest amount of pesticide residue-the Dirty Dozen-as well as a list of the fifteen kinds ofproduce that have the least amount of pesticide residue-the Clean Fifteen.

THE DIRTY DOZEN	THE CLEAN FIFTEEN
• The 2016 Dirty Dozen includes the following produce. These are considered among the year's most important produce to buy organic:	• The least critical to buy organically are the Clean Fifteen list. The following are on the 2016 list:

THE DIRTY DOZEN

Strawberries	Spinach
Apples	Tomatoes
Nectarines	Bell peppers
Peaches	Cherry tomatoes
Celery	Cucumbers
Grapes	Kale/collard greens
Cherries	Hot peppers

• *The Dirty Dozen list contains two additional itemskale/collard greens and hot peppers-because they tend to contain trace levels of highly hazardous pesticides.*

THE CLEAN FIFTEEN

Avocados	Papayas
Corn	Kiw
Pineapples	Eggplant
Cabbage	Honeydew
Sweet peas	Grapefruit
Onions	Cantaloupe
Asparagus	Cauliflower
Mangos	

• *Some of the sweet corn sold in the United States are made from genetically engineered (GE) seedstock. Buy organic varieties of these crops to avoid GE produce.*

APPENDIX 3: INDEX

Hey there!

Wow, can you believe we've reached the end of this culinary journey together? I'm truly thrilled and filled with joy as I think back on all the recipes we've shared and the flavors we've discovered. This experience, blending a bit of tradition with our own unique twists, has been a journey of love for good food. And knowing you've been out there, giving these dishes a try, has made this adventure incredibly special to me.

Even though we're turning the last page of this book, I hope our conversation about all things delicious doesn't have to end. I cherish your thoughts, your experiments, and yes, even those moments when things didn't go as planned. Every piece of feedback you share is invaluable, helping to enrich this experience for us all.

I'd be so grateful if you could take a moment to share your thoughts with me, be it through a review on Amazon or any other place you feel comfortable expressing yourself online. Whether it's praise, constructive criticism, or even an idea for how we might do things differently in the future, your input is what truly makes this journey meaningful.

This book is a piece of my heart, offered to you with all the love and enthusiasm I have for cooking. But it's your engagement and your words that elevate it to something truly extraordinary.

Thank you from the bottom of my heart for being such an integral part of this culinary adventure. Your openness to trying new things and sharing your experiences has been the greatest gift.

Catch you later,

Judy K. Silas

Printed in Great Britain
by Amazon

57966122R00044